RAISED-BED
GARDENING

Simon Akeroyd

RAISED-BED
GARDENING

How to Grow More
in Less Space

The Taunton Press

The Taunton Press, Inc., 63 South Main Street
P.O. Box 5506, Newtown, CT 06470-5506
e-mail: tp@taunton.com

Conceived, designed, and produced by
Quid Publishing
Part of The Quarto Group
Level 4 Sheridan House
114 Western Road
Hove BN3 1DD
www.quidpublishing.com

Illustrations by Joanna Kerr
Design by Ali Walper

Library of Congress Cataloging-in-Publication Data
In Progress

Printed in China

10 9 8 7 6 5 4 3 2 1

For Guy, Lissie, and Hugh

CONTENTS

PART 3: PLANTS AND PROJECTS

INTRODUCTION

Raised beds are not a new concept and the benefits of growing plants in them have been known for centuries. In fact, one of the earliest literary references was by a German Benedictine abbot called Walahfrid Strabo (c. 808–849) in his "Liber de cultura hortorum" (27 short poems praising gardening written in Latin hexameters), commonly known as the "Hortulus"('Little Garden'):

"I leave the whole plot to be baked, like a bun,
By the breath of the south wind and the heat of the sun.
Only, lest the soil slip and drift out of its place,
With four pieces of timber I edge the whole space,
And then heap up the bed on a gentle incline.
Next I rake till the surface is powdered and fine,
And lastly, to make its fertility sure,
I impose a thick mulch of well-rotted manure.
And now—a few vegetable seeds let us sow,
And watch how the older perennials grow."

Yet, despite not being a modern horticultural concept, raised beds are becoming increasingly popular, and in certain densely populated urban areas with limited growing space, they are almost essential if you should wish to grow your own food, or create an ornamental garden. This is due to the flexibility of the beds, being able to fit into tiny spaces, over concrete or paved areas, and if the existing garden has no soil, then this can be brought in and added to the bed.

The book is divided up into three easy-to-follow parts. The Basics takes you through the simple steps of creating a raised bed. It explains the benefits of building one, what tools and materials are required, and what they can be made from. It advises on where to position your raised bed so as to maximize the available sunlight. If the bed is going to be in shade or in frost pockets, there are plant suggestions to help you choose ones that are suitable. Finally, in this part there are tips on how to design a planting scheme to create exciting color or textural combinations and how to combat some of the more common pests and diseases.

The second part explains the different types of raised beds that can be constructed. It includes everything from buying "off-the-rack" products to building beds for free from recycled materials. It also explains some of the less well-known types of raised beds such as keyhole gardening, which is a type of sustainable raised bed popular in Africa, featuring a central compost heap and built from surrounding free materials, such as rocks dug out from the impoverished soil. Another type featured in this chapter, originating from Northern Europe and increasing in popularity around the rest of the world, is hugelkultur, involving building beds over rotting timber and tree stumps, which generates nutrients and improves the soil over time as it gradually decomposes.

One of the attractions of creating a raised bed is that you can do almost everything yourself, from building it right through to planting it. The third chapter, Plants and Projects, is packed full of suggestions on what you can either build or create in your own outdoor space. There are planting schemes to suit personal preferences ranging from Japanese gardens to vegetable plots or even a mini orchard. If you don't have a garden, then there are even projects for window boxes or green roof space.

This book will hopefully inspire you to try growing plants in raised beds. Whether you have a community garden space, a grand walled garden, or a tiny courtyard, raised beds can enhance and improve your outdoor space. Once you've started using them, you'll never look back.

Part 1:
THE BASICS

No matter what type of raised bed you have, there are some basic gardening principles that will help to ensure your plants are looking and performing at their best. This part of the book covers the basics, to get you up and running in the garden. It includes how to identify the best location for a raised bed, how to combat pests and diseases, and information on the best materials to use when constructing your raised bed.

WHY RAISED BEDS?

So what is so special about raised beds? Can they really transform your garden? After all, a raised bed is simply a flat bed that has been lifted up a bit. As soon as you start to apply the concept to your own garden, however, you will quickly realize their potential. There are almost as many variations on designs, materials, and techniques as there are plants that can be grown in them, and there are numerous advantages to planting in raised beds rather than directly in the ground.

Add interest

Gardens that are planted only at ground level can seem relatively flat and featureless. Raised beds change this, lifting the planting and immediately making the garden landscape visually more interesting. They provide a strong design element, and their size, shape, or design is only limited by your imagination.

Grow more

On a practical level, raised beds have improved drainage and their elevation means that they warm up faster in spring. This benefits the growth of your plants, particularly if you are growing food crops, and extends the growing season. Making a raised bed higher along one side than the other, so that the sloping side faces the sun, warms the bed even more effectively and promotes early growth.

Easier access

Creating a raised bed reduces the amount of bending involved in gardening, making the work less back-breaking and allowing you to appreciate the plants at closer quarters. This simply makes gardening more comfortable and enjoyable.

Save space and time

Raised beds are particularly well suited to urban gardens where space is limited. In a sloping garden, a series of raised beds will help to make the most of changes of level, and in a small garden, raised beds can be used to create the maximum planting space. A single, distinctive raised bed (such as a keyhole garden) also makes a good focal point, or even a good home for an attractive specimen plant. The reduced amount of weeding and labor required to maintain them suits our modern "time-poor" culture.

Raised beds are particularly well suited to urban gardens where space is limited.

Soil improvement

Where the soil is poor or unsuitable for growing certain types of plants, or if you have a patio garden and therefore no soil at all, raised beds are extremely useful—almost vital. They allow for massive improvement of the soil, and growing conditions can be tailored to the needs of particular plants, such as alpines and lime-intolerant plants. While this can be achieved in a large container, raised beds have a distinct advantage in that there is far more room for root development, and the soil dries out much less quickly and is less prone to fluctuations in temperature.

MAKING RAISED BEDS WORK FOR YOU

Raised beds are a wonderfully efficient method of gardening but they do have their own inherent challenges. Some advanced planning and awareness of the issues involved are required to ensure that raised beds work for you.

Practical considerations

Lifting materials to a raised height can be hard work and if done incorrectly can cause strain or even injury. For example, using a watering can is much easier when watering crops at a lower height, whereas lifting a full can up to raised bed height can be awkward. Of course, there are solutions to this, such as using irrigation systems or a hose and breakers. Lifting other heavy materials such as wheelbarrow loads of compost or heavy plants in pots can also be harder. However, you can use low ramps or scaffold boards to push small amounts of compost in on wheelbarrows. Alternatively, just use smaller, lighter containers such as buckets to lift materials.

How high is too high?

In raised beds, tall climbing plants such as French and runner beans or hops might actually end up being too tall for you to reach if you grow them up teepees and upright structures, meaning you then need to use ladders to harvest and tie in your crops. However, there are dwarf versions of these plants that are just as easy to grow and will make harvesting and maintenance very easy.

Budget

Construction costs for raised beds are much higher than when growing crops directly in the soil. Whether using bricks, rocks, or lumber, materials usually have to be bought. This is in addition to nails, screws, and the tools to put them together such as drills, jigsaws, and hammers. Then there are the costs of the planting material. In an ideal world, people would have a pile of home-made compost that could be used to fill the beds, but the reality is that most people will have to import material into the garden. However, the initial outlay is well worth it, because in the long term, the beds will

last for a good few years and will increase efficiency, with larger harvests for vegetable crops. In addition, raised beds should reduce the need for anti-slug and -snail measures, because the beds raise the produce further off the ground.

Retain moisture

Depending on what type of raised bed you choose, it could result in having to water the plants more regularly than ones grown in the ground during the growing period. This is because raised beds provide better drainage. However, solutions such as hugelkultur and keyhole gardening (see pages 72–79) provide improvements to the soil structure that help to retain moisture rather than losing it.

Allow adequate space

Constructing raised beds will reduce the amount of growing space you have outdoors. This is because you will need space to move between them. Ideally, the space should be at least wide enough to get a wheelbarrow between the beds, so this can result in losing invaluable planting areas to paths. The benefit, though, is that the raised bed will increase efficiency overall, and you can plant closer together due to the extra depth in your raised bed and the improved drainage. Reducing the amount of growing space could be an advantage if you are looking to simplify your garden or reduce the maintenance, or create some sort of structure to its layout.

To DIY or not to DIY?

There is nothing complicated about making a raised bed. Armed with a few basic tools, construction of a bed is very easy. Of course, you can employ a landscape gardener to construct them for you, or buy pre-built kits that you assemble yourself, but this will incur further costs.

Weeding and harvesting

Hand weeding is much easier at a raised height, but using a hoe can be tricky due to the angle, as can digging out deep perennial weeds with a fork. Crops that require digging up with a spade, such as Jerusalem artichokes and potatoes, can also be more awkward in raised beds. It is always best to avoid walking on the raised beds, so if you think you will need to dig over the soil then do consider the size and shape of the raised bed before you build it. Think carefully about which crops are practical to grow. Crops that require digging can instead be grown in compost bags, where the bags can be ripped open to harvest instead. Ideally, you want to work to measurements that allow you to reach all areas of the bed to weed or harvest efficiently. You can always use a hand fork, trowel, or hand hoe for digging, which can comfortably be done from the side of the raised bed.

CHOOSING MATERIALS

Almost any material can be used to construct a raised bed, as long as it is strong enough to retain soil. Avoid materials that could contaminate the soil and thereby affect the health of the plants and, potentially, humans. For example, the creosote and tar in old railroad ties can affect the soil, and materials such as asbestos are carcinogenic. The main factors that should guide you in making your choice are budget, the availability of materials, and personal taste.

Wood

Wood is reasonably cheap, readily available from home improvement centers, and it only requires basic DIY skills to construct a raised bed using it. Hardwood is more durable than softwood, although softwood that has been pressure treated will have increased longevity. Gravel boards are useful as they are light and strong and additional boards can be added to create more depth each year if more compost or soil is added. Railroad ties give a raised bed an attractive, chunky, rustic feel and provide a very sturdy structure. They are wide enough to also provide a seating area, which can be a useful platform to rest on after a session of digging or weeding the raised bed. Beware of using old recycled railroad ties, though, as they can leach out creosote and tar into the beds and contaminate the soil. You can buy new railroad ties, both hard- and softwood, from lumber merchants and they will cut them to size for you. Wooden pallets, logs, or old scaffold boards are also useful materials that can be used to construct raised beds. Pallets are often found outside garden centers, warehouses, and factories. Always check with the proprietor of the business before helping yourself. Tree surgeons and garden companies will often have surplus logs. Look on recycling websites for scaffold boards, or buy from home improvement centers. The main disadvantage of wood is that it will eventually rot and will need to be replaced. Bricks and metal will last far longer. You could consider reconstituted plastic in the style of wood, which will create a similar look to wood and have much better durability.

Bricks

Bricks are the ideal material to use for a raised bed.
A certain degree of bricklaying skill is required, and the
bed will require footings to prevent the walls from sinking,
and cappings on top to prevent water egression (see pages
28–29). But the effort will be worth it because they are hard-
wearing and your brick raised bed will last years. With a
bit of imagination they can be built into whatever shape is
required. There are different types of bricks in a range of
colors to choose from, but it is usually best to select ones that
are in keeping with the surroundings (unless you're trying
to make a statement). For example, if your house is made of
modern red brick then choose these for your raised bed.
If you have an old traditional cottage built of mellow yellow
bricks, then it might be worth hunting down local, reclaimed
bricks of the same color. The downside of using bricks is that
if you have to buy them, they can be expensive. Try looking
on local freecycling and community selling websites, as you
will often find second-hand bricks for sale.

Breeze blocks

These are larger and easier to lay than bricks. They can look
somewhat unrefined if left unrendered, but if this doesn't
concern you they are a good cheap alternative to bricks.

Rocks, stones, and flint

Materials from your garden such as rocks and
stones can be reused to build up the sides of beds.
Traditionally, artisan craftsmen create drystone or flint
walls using a lime-based mortar to hold them together.

Metal

A metal raised bed can look very chic and stylish in a contemporary garden. Recycled material can often be found and used. Try visiting local scrapyards to see what material they have. Almost anything can be used, from corrugated metal sheeting to old metal trash cans. A metal worker or engineering company can cut sheets of metal to any shape or size. Be aware that the metal will get hot in summer and the bed will require extra watering toward the sides. During winter the bed will be colder than ones made of wood or brick, which could be a problem if it is on a cold site.

Natural materials

Raised beds can also be created from stacks of sod, from soil molded into retaining walls, or from wattle and daub (see page 84). Straw bales have also become a popular choice for growing kitchen garden plants in (see pages 94–95). Woven material such as wicker or woven hazel or willow can be used to create a cottage garden feel and should last for a couple of years before needing to be replaced. Bear in mind that while natural materials can look very attractive, they often have a reduced life expectancy.

Willow edging panels

Raised beds made from willow panels make an attractive feature in traditional kitchen gardens and potagers. The panels should be attached to upright wooden stakes at each end of the panel, either with string or wire, or nailed into place. You can buy the panels online or from most garden centers. The material is completely natural and untreated and should last for a few years in the garden. Willow panels shouldn't be too high as they won't be strong enough to retain a large amount of soil: about 10 inches high and 4 feet long is ideal. If you're just growing annuals, you could take them down in winter, store them in the shed, and bring them outside again the following spring. This should help to prolong their lifespan. They can be used as raised beds in their own right, or they could be used to disguise an uglier material such as plastic by using them as "dressing" around the outside of it. If using them as a raised bed, then add a liner on the inside to help preserve their life.

Recycled materials

There are plenty of recycled materials that can be used to make a raised bed: anything from a rubber tire to an old sandpit. Old roof tiles or bricks can be pushed into the ground on their edges to create a low bed. Even the chassis and framework of a scrap car can be used to grow plants in.

HOW DEEP?

The depth required for your raised bed will depend on various factors: the type of plants you are intending to grow, and whether the bed is on a patio, has a bottom to it, or sits directly on the soil below. If the bed is directly on soil, then plants with larger roots will eventually grow through the depth of the raised bed and into the ground beneath, meaning that the height of the raised bed is less important.

Salad crops, annuals, and herbs

If you are planning on growing only a few salad crops each year, then about 4 inches is sufficient depth. Salad crops are very shallow rooting and will even produce decent leafy crops in a window box, so a deep raised bed is not essential. You may, of course, have other reasons for growing them in a higher raised bed, such as ease of maintenance, or for the sake of appearance. Annual bedding plants such as busy lizzie, petunia, lobelia, begonia, annual rudbeckia, and cosmos have similar requirements and won't produce large root systems, meaning they will thrive in shallow soil. Many perennial herbs, such as rosemary, mint, and thyme, originate from the Mediterranean region, where they happily grow in arid and rocky soil conditions, so they won't require a deep root run either.

Herbaceous perennials, deeper-rooted vegetables, and ornamental grasses

Herbaceous plants will have a much larger root system than annuals and therefore require a deeper raised bed. Vegetables such as carrots, potatoes, cabbages, peas, beans, and so on will also need a deeper root run. For most, a depth of at least 12 inches is needed to allow them to grow to their full potential. They will grow in more shallow conditions, but it may be necessary to feed and water them more to compensate for the lack of soil or compost.

Shrubs and fruit bushes

Most fruit bushes and shrubs will require at least 20 inches depth of soil to allow them to fully develop and grow. It is possible for them to grow in shallower conditions but their growth will be stunted considerably and they probably won't live as long as if they were planted in deeper soil.

Trees

As a rule of thumb, what you see above the ground is usually mirrored by the root system below the ground, so you can imagine the root system required for a large tree. Of course, trees are very adaptable, and you only have to look at bonsai trees to see how their growth can be curtailed to suit the available space. Some trees can be bought on dwarf rootstock, which reduces their overall size. However, ideally trees should be given at least 3-4 feet of depth in a raised bed.

SITING YOUR RAISED BED

The key to successful gardening is matching the right plants with the position of the raised bed. In small gardens, you may not have much choice as to where the beds are constructed, but thankfully there are plants to suit every aspect, whether it be a shady, damp corner or a dry, sun-baked bed.

Shady corners

If possible and space allows, it is best to select an open, sunny site. The majority of plants require maximum sunlight to thrive. With more of their leaves exposed to the sunlight, they produce more sugars, which sweetens the taste of any fruit or vegetables that they produce. However, if your garden is in the shade for most of the day, don't despair. Some plants are shade-loving: for example, leafy crops such as cabbages, spinach, and summer salads prefer it slightly cooler. The beds will also have less tendency to dry out from the sun and the cool root system will mean that vegetable plants are far less likely to bolt. There are also plenty of ornamental plants that thrive in shady corners, such as hostas, ferns, epimediums, and hellebores.

Check the light

Before building a raised bed it is a good idea to examine where the sunlight falls in the garden to maximize the sunlight. It may sound obvious, but do bear in mind, particularly in small gardens, that a flower bed that is in the sunlight on the ground might be moved slightly out of the light once it is raised. Tree canopies, walls, and roofs might suddenly block an area that is usually bathed in sunlight when directly on the ground.

Understanding the aspect

The sun rises in the east and sets in the west. In the middle of the day the sun is in the south. For this reason, south-facing raised beds will be much warmer and sunnier than those constructed on the north side of the house. Ideally, a raised bed should be in sunlight for as much of the day as possible. So if your back yard faces north, but you are lucky enough to have a spacious front yard, then consider constructing your raised bed there. Also, remember that the sun is much higher in summer than in winter, so if you are hoping to extend the season, do check to see whether your garden still receives sunlight when at its lowest height.

Creating more light

Another method of allowing more sunlight into your garden is to cut back overhanging and overgrown vegetation and branches. Consider asking your neighbors if they are happy to reduce the height of their boundaries or cut back some of the trees in their garden if it is affecting the light in your garden. Lowering your boundary fence could also allow more light in, although, of course, this could be at the cost of your privacy.

Location, location, location

You should also give practical issues consideration when deciding where to site your raised bed. If you are planning on growing vegetables or herbs, then you may wish to place it near the kitchen window or back door to make it as easy as possible to grab fresh produce when cooking. Perhaps you wish to create more privacy from your neighbors— raising the height of your garden on the boundaries by placing raised beds there will help with this. They can also be placed around a patio or seating area to create a sense of privacy. If you are planning to grow tall plants in your raised bed, it's best not to site it near to the house as it could end up blocking your view of the garden.

Providing shelter

Like human beings, plants often prefer some protection from the elements. Exposure to the wind can decimate the leaves on plants. Furthermore, it can cause plants to quickly dry out as it sucks away any moisture in the soil. Strong winds during blossoming season will cause low yields in fruit trees and bushes, as pollinating insects are unable to fly in windy weather. One of the solutions is to choose tough, tenacious plants that will tolerate the wind. Most plants that thrive in coastal locations are suitable. However, if you wish to grow tender plants or even most types of vegetables, some protection from the wind is required. Most small gardens, particularly in towns, will already have adequate shelter from winds as they will be surrounded by hedges, walls, and fences. In larger gardens it is best to avoid creating raised beds in exposed conditions such as on top of a hill. The best type of windbreak is a hedge, since it slows down the excessive blasts of wind, but is semipermeable, meaning that there is still some air circulation. This is important as it helps to prevent the build-up of pests and diseases, particularly fungus, which thrive in stagnant, still conditions.

Non-permeable structures such as walls and fences will prevent some wind damage, but they can also have a detrimental effect, as sometimes the wind can buffer along the top edge and drop down onto the raised bed with extra strength.

Frost pockets

Many plants will suffer if you place your raised bed in a frost pocket. Frost generally collects in the lowest part of the garden, as the cold air drifts into it, replacing any warmer air that rises. The effect is often exacerbated if the cold air is prevented from circulating by a permanent structure, such as a wall or fence at the lowest end of the garden. Young seedlings will quickly get zapped by the cold weather, while young, tender shoots or blossoms will shrivel up and die. It will reduce the length of the available growing season too, as the soil will be too cold to sow anything until late spring, and plants will quickly die back in fall. Avoiding cold, frosty sites will allow early spring sowings and extend the season well into the following late autumn. If it is not possible to avoid a frost pocket, then be prepared to cover plants and sow later in the season to avoid the disappointment of losing your plants to a harsh frost.

Raised beds can be placed around a patio or seating area to create a sense of privacy.

BASIC CONSTRUCTION OF A WOODEN RAISED BED

There are many different ways to create a wooden raised bed but the guidelines below provide a simple outline of the basic construction methods.

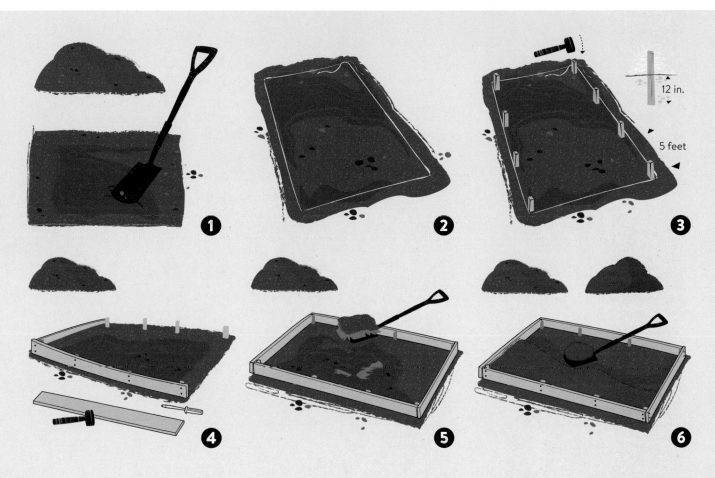

1 | *If the soil where the raised bed is to be constructed is of good quality, then this should be removed and saved for later to top off the bed.*

2 | *Use string to mark out the perimeter of the bed.*

3 | *Raised beds will require retaining stakes that are 2 inches by 2 inches wide that should be banged into the corners using a sledge hammer. The sides will also require support, with stakes placed every 5 feet. Drive these approximately 12 inches into the ground.*

4 | *Next, attach the retaining wooden boards to the stakes using galvanized screws.*

5 | *Fill up the lower section of the raised bed with soil. If you had to remove grass where the bed was to be constructed, this can be placed upside down in the bottom as it will gradually rot over the season.*

6 | *Top off the bed with a 50:50 mix of topsoil and garden compost/general purpose compost.*

SOIL GUIDE

To save money on topsoil, reserve any soil dug from the garden when constructing paths or patio areas and use to top off the raised bed. If buying soil for the raised bed garden, make sure you get exactly what you need so your garden is successful. There are different types of garden soil commonly available.

Garden soil is usually a mix of topsoil, peat moss, sphagnum moss, and, possibly, slow-release fertilizer.

Compost in many forms is available, including composted animal manures such as cow, chicken, or rabbit, and composted plant materials. The bags should be marked as to the contents.

Topsoil is usually medium-poor soil that has been scraped off of building sites. It can be used as filler, but should always be mixed with garden soil or compost for the best result.

BASIC CONSTRUCTION OF A BRICK RAISED BED

Brick raised beds are harder to build than wooden ones, requiring slightly more practical skills, such as bricklaying, but nothing too difficult to learn. They should last a lifetime once constructed and provide a strong, sturdy bed that looks great in most locations, whether it be a garden or a front or back yard.

HOW TO CUT A BRICK

1 | Make a slight groove in the middle of the brick with the edge of a trowel.

2 | Put a brick bolster into the groove and bang down sharply with a hammer. The brick should break cleanly in two. Remember to put on protective eyewear when splitting bricks.

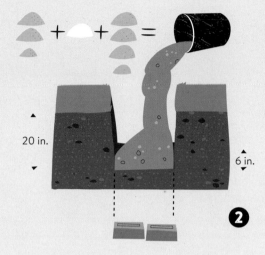

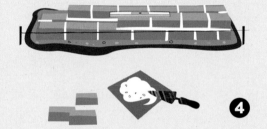

1 | Use string to mark out the perimeter of the bed.

2 | Construct a concrete footing. This will prevent the bed from sinking. Dig out a trench 20 inches deep and the width of two bricks. Line the bottom with a concrete foundation (one part cement, two and a half parts sand, three and a half parts gravel) to a depth of 6 inches. Leave to dry.

3 | Mix up your cement, using three parts sand to one part cement. Water should be added to make it an easy-to-use consistency that isn't too sloppy but is flexible enough to spread onto the brickwork. Adding plasticizer will help keep the cement flexible.

4 | Start to lay the courses of bricks, two bricks wide. Bed each brick onto a 1 inch layer of cement. Start the second layer with half a brick so that the bricks are staggered with the courses below it, as this will make it stronger. Use strings and a level to ensure that each course is level.

5 | The first three layers will take you up to ground level. Continue above ground level until you reach your desired height.

6 | Pairs of chamfered coping bricks should be cemented all around the top edge for protection from dampness and to make it look more attractive.

7 | Line the inside of the walls with a permeable membrane.

8 | Add topsoil and compost (see points 5–6, page 26).

PATHS

If you are planning on having more than one raised bed, you need to think carefully about the paths that will lead around and between them. Paths form the backbone and structure to any garden design and are essential in ensuring that the key elements of the garden can be reached. They need to be functional and practical, but ideally should also look good and fit in with the style of your raised bed. For example, a formal brick raised bed may look incongruous with a rustic woodchip path around it.

Bricks or paving slabs

The most solid paths are constructed of bricks or paving slabs and will provide a sturdy base to push your wheelbarrow along. For a rustic look, they can simply be laid into the soil, digging them down to the depth of the brick or patio slab so that they are flush with the ground. If you prefer, you can bed them on sand and then brush in a dry mix of sand and cement to keep them more secure. Lightly water it to let the mix set. They come in a range of sizes and prices to suit most people's budgets. If you aren't worried about style, then check in dumpsters, as very often you will find people chucking out old bricks and paving slabs. Of course, you should always check with the house owner or builder before rummaging through their dumpster.

Grass

This is the cheapest option. However, it will also require the most maintenance as it will need mowing once a week during the growing season. The edges will also need strimming regularly if the grass is laid right up to the sides of the raised bed. If the beds cast shade over the grass paths, then a shade-tolerant mix of grass seed will be required to keep the grass green all year long.

HOW WIDE?

In order for you to be able to comfortably walk between your raised beds, the path between them should be at least 16 inches wide. If you wish to push a wheelbarrow along the path, it should be at least 26 inches wide. For wheelchair access, the recommended width for one wheelchair to pass with no room alongside is 3.4 feet (for a wheelchair plus a pedestrian alongside it's 5 feet).

Woodchip mulch

This is a relatively cheap option. To create one, gravel boards should be placed on either side of the path and held in place with wooden pegs. Gravel boards are usually ¾ inch wide, 6 inches high and 6 or 8 feet long. These boards will help to retain the woodchip mulch on the path and prevent it from spreading onto the lawns and other flower beds. Next, a layer of ground-suppressing membrane should be laid on the path and held down with metal tent pegs. Finally, cover the path with a layer of woodchip mulch 2 inches deep and rake it level. The woodchip mulch will need topping off regularly as it washes away or rots.

Gravel

Gravel paths are reasonably cheap and straightforward to construct. One of the downsides is that if you drop compost or soil onto it, it is hard to gather up and tidy away. The base of the path should be dug out to approximately 6 inches deep. Use treated lumber to create the edges of the path and prevent the gravel spreading onto other areas. Drive in wooden pegs at 3 foot intervals to hold the edging in place. Compact down the ground using a wacker plate or roller. Alternatively, if the path only covers a small area, you could tread it flat. Place a layer of hardcore in the base of the path, then a layer of sand, then top off with a 2 inch layer of gravel and rake and roll it.

Constructing a herringbone brick path

For a simple rustic effect in your garden, a herringbone path can be constructed between the raised beds.

1 | *To ensure the path is flush with the surface, dig out the soil where the path is to be laid to a depth of 1 inch more than the depth of the bricks you will be using.*

2 | *Place a layer of sand in the bottom of the path to a thickness of 1 inch.*

3 | *Lay the bricks in a herringbone pattern along the length of the path.*

4 | *Use a sledge hammer to bed the bricks into the sand and then brush more sand into the gaps between the cracks.*

PLANNING YOUR RAISED BED

A good planting scheme requires planning. In fact, more time should be spent on selecting and choosing the correct plants than the actual process of planting itself. It is important to decide on the look that you require and then research the plants' requirements.

WHAT TYPE OF PLANTS WILL YOU GROW?

WATER PLANTS	
BEDDING PLANTS AND ANNUALS	
HERBACEOUS BORDERS	
SHRUBS	
FRUIT BUSHES	
TREES	
VEGETABLES	
ALPINES	
HERBS	
GRASSES AND BAMBOOS	

To the drawing board

The best way to start is to draw out your plan on a piece of graph paper, plotting which plants are going to be placed where. This will save you making expensive mistakes at a garden center by buying too many plants. If you are planning on growing vegetables in the raised beds, then it will be necessary to methodically plot which vegetables will grow where, to ensure plants are given the right amount of space and that taller plants won't be shading smaller ones. You may need more than one raised bed so that you can rotate your crops each year (see crop rotation, page 56). If you are planning an ornamental display, then you will need to ensure that the plants you have chosen are suitable for the soil and climate conditions.

Say it with color

In an ornamental bed, you will also need to think about how the plants combine in terms of color. You could consider planting a single-color theme in the raised bed. Alternatively, you may wish to select colors that will create a certain mood, such as bright, vibrant, hot colors or calming, tranquil, pastel colors. Some garden designers find it useful to use a color wheel to decide which colors work well together and which colors will clash.

DESIGN THEORY

Color doesn't have to be the only aesthetic focus in your raised bed. You could play around with texture, movement or height, such as creating a bed full of ornamental grasses and bamboos.

Color wheel

A color wheel is a useful tool for working out which color combinations work well. As a rule of thumb, colors that sit alongside each other on the wheel, such as green and yellow, will be a harmonious and calm combination, whereas plants of colors completely opposite each other on the wheel, such as yellow and purple, are a striking combination, creating a bigger impact.

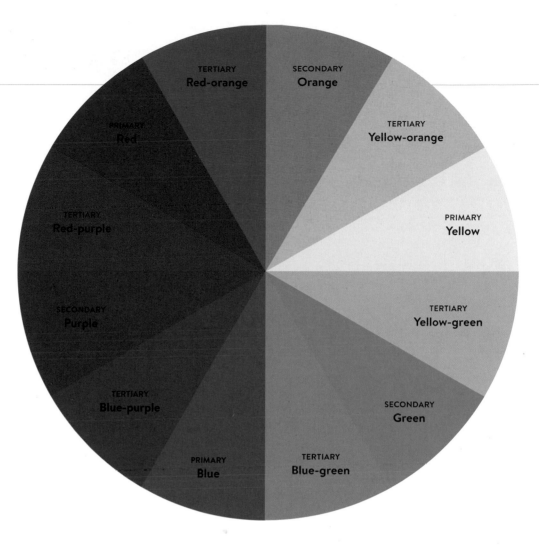

Size matters

When you are designing a bed situated directly on the ground, the rules of placement according to the plants' size are fairly simple: tall plants at the back, shorter ones at the front. However, raised beds are slightly different as they are viewed from different angles. Think about how the bed is going to be seen. If your raised bed will have a path running around its entirety, it will be seen from all sides. As a rule of thumb, it is best to place taller plants in the middle and smaller ones at the edge. Bear in mind, though, that taller plants will shade the plants next to them as the sun moves across the sky, so think carefully about which plants you place next to them. In a vegetable bed, you could consider planting shade-tolerant plants such as lettuce and other leafy vegetables next to the taller plants. Avoid in such places sun-loving plants such as tomatoes, pumpkins, and squashes, and remember that plants such as carrots and potatoes need at least half a day of sunshine.

THE ANSWER LIES IN THE SOIL

Having the right soil conditions is essential if you want your plants to perform at their best. Some plants have very specific requirements in terms of the level of acidity or alkalinity that they will thrive in, though most garden plants prefer neutral conditions and will tolerate slightly acidic or alkaline variations. It is worth checking the pH level of your soil first in case it is extremely acidic or alkaline.

ACIDIC-SOIL-LOVING PLANTS INCLUDE…	ALKALINE-SOIL-LOVING PLANTS INCLUDE…
HOLLIES	CEANOTHUS
PRIMULAS	LAVENDER
RHODODENDRONS	CLEMATIS
AZALEAS	DIANTHUS
MAPLES	GERANIUM
MAGNOLIAS	CAMPANULA
CAMELLIAS	LIGUSTRUM
BLUEBERRIES	BUDDLEJA
CRANBERRIES	CHOISYA

Soil testing kits are very easy to use and will quickly identify which plants your soil or compost will suit.

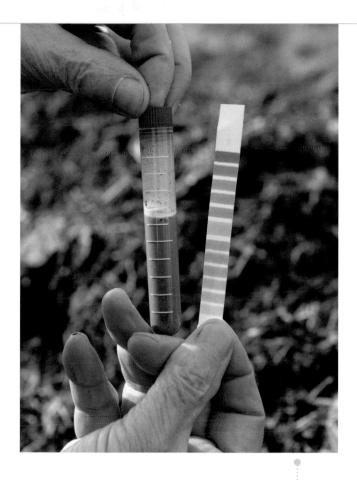

Know your soil

Simple soil testing kits can be bought online or from most garden centers. They are very easy to use and will allow you to quickly identify which plants your soil or compost will suit. A sample of soil or compost is shaken up in a testing solution and the color the liquid changes to is then checked on the color chart. 1 is extremely acidic and 14 is extremely alkaline. A pH of 7 is neutral. It is advisable to take a few samples from different areas of the raised bed to make sure an accurate reading is being taken.

Acid soil

Adding compost to the soil can lower the pH so that it is more acidic. If your soil is on the alkaline side and you want to grow acid-loving plants, this step is necessary, and, in most gardens, this enough. Make your own acidic compost at home by adding lots of rotted pine needles, woodchips, sawdust, rotting leaves, or even fresh coffee grounds to the compost pile. It will eventually turn neutral again, so it is worth checking every year and topping off with more acidic materials if needed. There are also acidifying products that can be bought from garden suppliers. Sulphur is the most common product used to acidify the soil, sulphur dust being quicker to acidify the soil than sulphur chips. It only acidifies the soil once it has been broken down by microorganisms, so results are not instantaneous. It can take weeks before conditions are acidic enough to suit the plants' requirements.

Alkaline soil

Adding mushroom compost or hardwood ash to the compost can be an effective method of creating more alkaline conditions. Alternatively, there are products that can be bought such as ground limestone, commonly called 'garden lime', which has the active ingredient of calcium carbonate. Calcified seaweed and ground chalk also provide calcium carbonate. Dolomite lime is a ground limestone that provides magnesium carbonate and calcium carbonate. Gardeners often use it to lime soils that are lacking magnesium. Always follow the manufacturer's instructions if using these products. Do remember that watering with soft or hard water can also affect the pH of the compost in your raised bed. The material used to construct the beds could gradually have a leaching effect on the soil too. For example, fresh pine or treated wood could make it acidic near the edges of the bed.

Work with your soil

Remember that anything you add to the soil in order to affect the pH balance is only a temporary solution, and the best advice is to work with your soil type rather than attempting to change it—a much more economical solution that will also have a much smaller environmental impact. Significantly changing a soil's pH for any length of time is not a very easy thing to do, unless you import soil.

GETTING READY FOR PLANTING

It's all in the preparation! Whether your plants thrive or struggle in their raised bed is largely down to how well you prepare the soil before planting. Planting a raised bed is very similar to planting a flower border or vegetable patch when growing in normal conditions. However, plants are occasionally planted closer together in a raised bed, particularly in deep beds, as it is assumed roots will go further downwards.

Groundwork

The soil or compost should be prepared thoroughly before beginning to plant. All plants have different requirements for growing—such as spacing between plants, sunlight and

moisture, and soil type—and some are more particular than others. There is usually information on the packet of seeds or plant label which you can check if you're unsure.

If plants have been grown in the soil before, dig it over and remove any perennial weeds. It is usually best not to walk on raised beds to avoid compacting the soil, but depending on the height and width of the bed, it may be possible to lay planks or scaffold boards across the bed in order to access the soil, assuming the raised bed is strong enough to take the weight. If vegetables are to be planted, then the soil will benefit from having well-rotted manure or garden compost added. Dig this in, rake the soil level, and allow it to settle for a few days.

Filling up

Don't overfill your beds. Although the soil level will gradually drop slightly, if beds are filled above the edge of the bed, then soil and water will spill out. Aim to have the level of the soil about 1-3 inches below the top of the bed. The levels can always be topped off with mulch or compost later in the year. In fact, you'll probably want to add mulch or compost each year to improve the soil, so leaving a gap for this is a good idea.

If climbing structures are required for plants such as runner beans, climbing roses, or clematis, then it is best to get these in place first to avoid trampling over the plants at a later date. Climbing structures can include teepees, trellises, or archways.

Planting out

Before planting anything into the raised bed it is best to give the plants a good watering first. Sit the plants in trays, water the soil until saturated, and then leave them in the trays to soak up any more water if needed for about an hour. Prepare a planting hole in the bed prior to removing each plant from its pot to reduce the time the root ball is exposed to daylight and thereby minimize its chances of drying out. Once the planting hole is dug, the plant should be eased out of its pot. If the plant is rootbound, the roots should be teased out to prevent them from continuing to spiral around once planted, as this will eventually strangle the plant. This is more important with trees and shrubs as they have a longer life expectancy than herbaceous plants and will therefore be more affected.

Most trees and shrubs should not be planted any deeper in the ground than they were in the pot. It's also important to ensure that the plants are at the correct planting distance from each other. If you are unsure, then check the plant label. The key is that once the plants have grown to their correct height a minimal amount of soil is left exposed. This is because bare soil will enable weeds to germinate and the rain and wind will cause any nutrients to leach out.

WATERING

Plants grown in raised beds will require more watering than plants grown directly in the ground due to the extra drainage the raised beds provide. The extra warmth of a raised bed and exposure to wind will also cause the soil to dry out faster. In summer it is particularly important that plants are kept well watered, otherwise they will rapidly start wilting and possibly even die. In fact, lack of water is the number one reason for plants dying in the garden. However, there are a few methods of reducing the amount of water that the plants will need.

Mulch

Try to avoid leaving soil exposed in the raised bed as moisture will quickly evaporate. Instead, cover it over with mulch such as garden manure. Digging organic matter into the soil will also help retain moisture.

Choose drought-tolerant plants

Choose plants that will cope with dry conditions. Many ornamental plants, including grasses, bamboos, and modern-style North American prairie plants, will tolerate dry conditions. Herbs are also fairly drought tolerant.

Irrigation

Consider using irrigation in the garden but avoid sprinklers, as these throw a lot of water in the air and very often don't hit the target. Instead, use soaker hoses which lie on the surface of the raised bed in among the plants and gently trickle out water around the root system. They can be placed on timers so they only produce water for short amounts of time. A home-made soaker hose can easily be made by puncturing an old hose with tiny holes using a fork.

Timing

Avoid watering plants in the middle of the day. This can result in the water evaporating before it has had a chance to percolate down into the roots. It can also cause leaf scorch if wet leaves get caught by the midday sun. Watering is most effective in the evening (although the prolonged dampness during the evening can encourage slugs) or in the morning.

Water sumps

Build up small mounds of soil in a ring around a plant to create a sort of bowl that you can then fill with water. This holds the water in place around the roots, ensuring that it doesn't drain off away from the plant.

Accuracy

If possible, avoid watering with a hose as water can be lost due to excess splashing. Very often it doesn't accurately target the root system, instead splashing over the leaves, flowers, and surrounding areas. If feasible, use a watering can and specifically target the area around the roots.

Harvesting rainwater

During the summer staying on top of watering is essential. With environmental concerns and the costly implications of water meters for some people, it is advisable to harvest as much rainwater as possible to use in the garden. It seems a shame to watch all that rainwater washing away down the storm drain, and then having to pay for it out of the spigot. Rain barrels can be installed to collect the rain that is funnelled along guttering coming off roofs. Guttering can easily be attached to any buildings or structures in the garden such as a greenhouse or shed.

1 | *Use a tape measure to work out how much plastic guttering is going to be required to go all the way around the structure to capture all the rainwater.*

2 | *Next, use a pencil to mark on the shed where the rain barrel is going to go. This is where the outlet for the guttering will need to be placed. The rain barrel can be placed anywhere around the shed, usually to the side—just ensure that the doors can still be opened.*

3 | *Stretch a string around the shed as a guideline to work out where the guttering is going to start and where it will finish (by the water outlet), ensuring there is a very slight tilt so that rainwater drains away.*

4 | *Drill pilot holes into the side of the shed and screw gutter brackets to support the gutter at 3 foot intervals.*

5 | *Both ends of the guttering should have end pieces slotted on to prevent rainwater flowing out of the ends. Then clip the guttering into the bracket.*

6 | *Place the rain barrel underneath the gutter outlet. It should be raised up off the ground, for example using bricks, so that a watering can fits under the tap towards the bottom of the barrel.*

7 | *Use a tape measure to work out the distance from the guttering outlet to the top of the rain barrel and cut a downpipe accordingly.*

8 | *Connect the downpipe to the gutter outlet at the top and the rain barrel lid at the bottom. Attach the downpipe to the shed with a bracket.*

9 | *Finally, once the rain barrel has filled during winter it is a good idea to have a second one, and even a third, that will capture excess water from the first barrel. To do this, an outlet pipe can be attached to the downpipe to collect surplus water. The water will naturally flow into the adjacent rain barrel once the first barrel is full.*

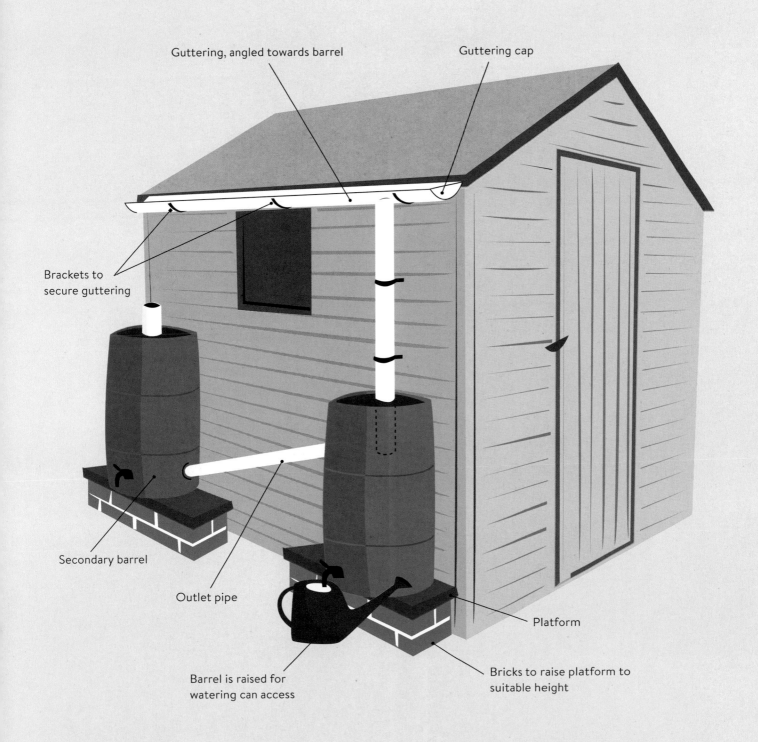

Guttering, angled towards barrel

Guttering cap

Brackets to secure guttering

Secondary barrel

Outlet pipe

Barrel is raised for watering can access

Platform

Bricks to raise platform to suitable height

COMPOSTING

Every good garden needs a good composting system, and it doesn't need to be complicated or high tech either. Not only is it free, you don't have to drive to the garden center to transport it in bulky bags and your home-made compost will probably be better and more natural than any product you can buy. Composting is a fantastic way of recycling kitchen and garden waste, and the resulting healthy, nutrient-rich compost can be added to the soil in your raised beds. There are lots of different types of composting systems available, including keyhole and hugelkultur (see pages 72–79), which rely on the natural decomposition of plant material to feed the raised bed. Compost bins can either be incorporated as part of the raised bed, or can be in a separate area of the garden.

How many bins?

If space allows, three compost heaps are ideal in a garden (though two is workable): one for adding waste to, one which is in the process of being left to rot, and a third which is already rotted and is to be used on the raised beds.

Keep the compost covered to prevent the material washing and leaching away. However, check on the heap to ensure it isn't drying out. If it is, then add water to the heap.

Turning the heap

Ideally, compost heaps should be turned monthly with a fork to enable air to get into the material, which will speed up the process of decomposition. However, it is not essential—you could turn it once a year, it will just take longer for the material to decompose. If possible, place an empty compost bay next to the heap, so that it can be turned into the empty bay and left.

Types of compost bins

Drum
The most common type of compost bin is the large plastic drum type, with an access hatch at the bottom and a lid.

Tumblers
Some compost bins have a rotating drum which saves you having to turn over the compost material with a fork.

Recycled containers
Any container can be used to hold compost. Some gardeners use woven bulk bags, while others use stacks of rubber tires, adding additional tires onto the stack as more compost is produced.

Troubleshooting

Getting a good quality compost is all about getting the right balance between the two main ingredients, carbon and nitrogen. Ideally, the balance should be two parts carbon to one part nitrogen. Carbon is supplied by material such as newspaper, dry leaves, wood chips, and bark. Nitrogen comes from green material such as grass clippings or green garden waste such as herbaceous plant material. If the compost is smelly and slimy then there is probably too much nitrogen in it and more carbon material should be added and mixed in. If the compost is too dry and not rotting then there is too much carbon and more green waste should be added. Water from the rain barrel can also be added.

An ideal mix for the majority of plants to grow in a raised bed is 50 percent topsoil and 50 percent garden compost, although more specialized plants such as alpines or acidic-soil-loving plants will have different requirements.

The compost is ready when it has rotted down into a dark brown, crumbly material and has a pleasant earthy, woodland aroma. It shouldn't smell unpleasant or feel excessively moist and slimy.

AVOID!

Don't add meat and cooked food to your compost heap. They won't rot properly and will attract rodents, as will unwashed eggshells. Never add roots from perennial weeds such as bindweed, knotweed, or ground elder, as they will quickly spread throughout the rotting material and from there into your raised beds when the compost gets used in the garden.

Pallet compost bin

Recycled pallets are very popular material for constructing compost bins. They are free —check with local factories, warehouses, and retail outlets for any surplus pallets. They are easy to make into a bin and the gaps between the slats allow air to circulate through the heap. Pallet bins can be attached to the back of raised beds as an additional feature, meaning you don't have to move the compost far when it's needed.

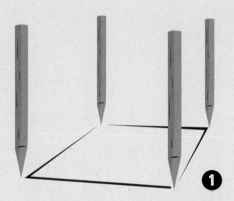

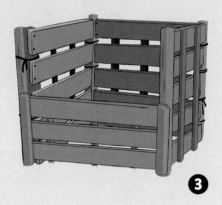

1 | *Bang in four stout upright posts to form the corners of the compost bin. They should be the same distance apart as the width of the pallet.*

2 | *Select three pallets of the same size, place them on their sides to form the back and sides of the compost heap and nail or tie them to the upright posts.*

3 | *Cut a fourth pallet in half and attach one section of it to the front. This will help to retain the material, yet is low enough to allow easy access to the heap.*

Liquid lunch

There are various fertilizers that can be added to your raised bed to boost the plants' health, speed of growth, and production of flowers and fruit. The simplest natural fertilizer, though, can be made easily from plants in the garden, particularly comfrey or nettles.

- Harvest comfrey or nettle leaves and place them into a bucket of water. Place a brick onto the leaves to hold them under the water.

- Leave them to "brew" for a few weeks—be warned, they do smell unpleasant when they're starting to break down.

- Filter the liquid through a sieve to remove any unrotted leaves. Use a funnel to decant the liquid into plastic milk cartons or bottles to store.

- Dilute this comfrey or nettle concentrate in a watering can at a ratio of ten parts water to one part liquid feed when using to feed the plants. Use once or twice every two weeks to give your herbaceous plants and vegetables a nitrogen-rich boost during the growing season.

Once you have filled your raised beds with compost and soil they won't need digging again for the first year.

To dig or not to dig

Once you have filled your raised beds with compost and soil they won't need digging again for the first year. However, in the second year, you will need to consider whether to dig over the beds thoroughly or leave them "undug."

In the world of gardening, opinions are divided. Traditionalists believe that the soil should be dug over before planting, the theory being that it breaks up any compaction and clods of earth, exposes pests to the cold weather and to predators such as birds and hedgehogs, removes the roots of weeds, and encourages deeper rooting of plants. However, there is a school of thought that believes digging over the ground damages soil structure, disturbs beneficial bugs in the soil, and encourages weed seed to germinate. Instead, they advocate adding layers of organic matter and mulch over the existing soil, allowing the rain or worms to take it down into the soil.

PESTS AND DISEASES

Unfortunately, there are many pests and diseases that can strike the plants in your raised bed at any time. One of the best methods of combating pests and diseases is to ensure that your plants are as strong, healthy, and resilient as possible. The other is to know the warning signs that pests or diseases are at work, and to react quickly. This section will take you through some of the prevalent threats to watch out for.

Keeping on top of things

If your plants are unhealthy, lacking in nutrients or water, or not growing in the correct environment, their immune systems will be weak and they will be far more susceptible to attack from fungus and pests. They will be less able to fight back and react by producing more growth. Here are a few things you can do to ensure your plants are in tip-top fighting form:

- ☑ *Keep plants well fed and watered.*

- ☑ *Build up a population of beneficial insects and predators by having a wildlife-friendly garden with ponds, mixed hedges, and a wide variety of plants. Even in a small garden, a bowl of water and a range of plants in containers and window boxes will help to encourage wildlife. This will encourage bugs such as ladybugs and lacewings that will feed on aphids, and birds and hedgehogs that will prey on slugs.*

- ☑ *Consider using biological controls—for example, nematodes can be used to combat snails on hostas, or vine weevil in containers.*

- ☑ *Choose varieties that have known resistance to a certain problem—for example, the carrot variety 'Flyaway' has resistance to carrot fly.*

- ☑ *Some gardeners believe that "companion planting," or growing certain plants next to each other, can have mutual benefits. Carrots and onions are often planted together because onion fly are deterred by the scent of carrots and carrot fly are likewise repelled by the scent of onions.*

- ☑ *Maintain good plant hygiene by ensuring that air can circulate around the plants and avoid planting too densely. Clear away fallen leaves, rotting fruit, and remove infected material from the plant as soon as it is spotted.*

Pests

Here are some of the more common pests that can be found in the garden. If you are working hard to grow delicious fruit or vegetables, it will be worth taking a few preventative measures to ensure that it is you who dines on them and not any of these creatures. Chemical controls can, of course, be used and are readily available from garden centers. However, there are non-chemical methods that are also worth trying, which will have a less detrimental side effect on the environment.

Slugs

Slugs happily munch through young plants and seedlings, and disappointed gardeners can find their entire vegetable crop devoured in just a few nights if left unmanaged. One of the benefits of growing vegetables in raised beds is that the plants are further off the ground and out of the reach of slugs and snails. The elevation will mean fewer of these pests, but it won't stop them entirely. It will also mean they are out of the reach of hedgehogs, one of the main natural predators of slugs, though the raised height will make the slugs more accessible to birds.

Slugs that do make it into your raised bed will tend to cluster around the sides and edges, so by keeping a regular vigilant watch you should be able easily to pick them off and dispose of them in whichever way you see fit. Another method is to make a beer trap. This involves sinking a container into the ground so that the top of the container is level with the soil, and filling it with beer. The theory is that the slug drinks the beer and then cannot get out and drowns. If you don't like the idea of wasting beer, then any other sugary solution should be enticing enough to capture them. Alternatively, you can scatter orange and grapefruit peels around the garden to attract the slugs, making them much easier to gather up in the evening.

Slugs prefer moist conditions, so water your plants early in the morning rather than the evening, when slugs begin to emerge.

Grit, eggshells, and other coarse materials can be scattered around a plant to prevent slugs and snails from crossing over to feast on them. Copper barrier tape can be bought from garden centers to place around plants. The material gives a slight electric shock to these pests to keep them at bay. They also try to avoid salt as it dehydrates them, leading to an unpleasant death. Seaweed can be used to create a barrier due to its salty content.

By far the most effective option, however, is slug pellets. Aluminium sulphate pellets are thought to be more environmentally friendly. Use them sparingly, to reduce the likelihood of them causing harm to animals. Just a few pellets around each plant should be sufficient. Seedlings and newly planted plants are the most vulnerable, and it is only these that will really need protection.

Birds

Birds can be beneficial in the garden and can help keep levels of small grubs and aphids down to a manageable level. However, the reality is that they will also enjoy munching on your crops—not so much of a problem, of course, if you're only growing ornamentals. Pigeons are particularly fond of brassicas such as cabbages, kale, and sprouts, while bullfinches will peck out the ripening buds on fruit trees. And most birds will help themselves to any ripening fruit. The best way to keep your crops safe from birds is to cover them with a bird net. Thankfully, growing crops in raised beds makes it easier to cover them as there is already a base to the structure. A basic protective fruit cage can simply be made by lashing together bamboo canes to create a 6 foot structure above the raised bed. Remember to peg down the bottom of the net to prevent birds from sneaking in underneath.

A specifically designed bird-scaring humming line can also be used as a deterrent over a raised bed. It should be tied tightly between two posts, which will cause it to hum in the wind, deterring the birds from visiting your crops.

Aphids

Aphids are a common pest found on plants, often on new shoots and leaves. They can be removed simply by washing them off with soapy water. If caught early enough, they shouldn't have too much detrimental effect on the plants. An alternative method of controlling them is to buy ladybug or lacewing larvae and release them near the plants. The larvae feed on the aphids, quickly clearing up the problem for you. Some birds will also feed on aphids.

Cabbage white butterfly/caterpillar

These butterflies lay eggs on members of the cabbage family and the hatched caterpillars then feed on the leaves. Cover the plants with a fine mesh to prevent the adult insects landing on the plants.

Cabbage root fly

Larvae of the root fly feed on the roots of cabbages. You can buy specially made discs from garden centers to place around the base of the stem and prevent the root fly from landing and laying eggs.

Carrot fly

These flies are attracted by the scent of the carrot. Their tiny maggot offspring tunnel into the roots of both carrots and parsnips. To prevent attack, choose resistant varieties or cover them with a fine mesh to keep the tiny flies off your plants.

Japanese beetle

Japanese beetles will feed on the leaves of plants at any age. To control them you need to eliminate their larval form—the grubs. Visit your local garden center for *Bacillus thuringiensis* or Milky spore to apply to the lawn to eliminate the grubs.

Deer, woodchucks, and chipmunks

Deer, woodchucks, and chipmunks can all lay waste to a garden with astonishing efficiency. Sometimes they'll eat an entire plant to the ground, while other times they'll take a bite or two out of every single flower or fruit on the vine. Protect young trees by caging them with chicken wire. Sink the cage at least 12 inches into the ground, as woodchucks will burrow. Spray repellents on annuals, perennials, shrubs, vegetables, and small fruits to prevent deer, woodchucks, and chipmunks from munching.

Mice and rats

Rodents love to feed on the seeds that you have just planted out, particularly peas and bean seeds. They will also feed on fruit, and they love sweetcorn. Traps can be placed to catch mice. There are poisons that can be used for rat infestations and advice can be sought from pest control companies.

Common diseases

There are many diseases that can affect the health of your plants. The trick is to try to catch the problem early to prevent it from spreading. Good plant hygiene and keeping your plant healthy are among the best methods of avoiding diseases, ensuring that they are strong enough to combat the problem if an attack should occur.

Powdery mildew

Gooseberry, squash, and blackcurrant plants are very susceptible to this fungus, which causes the leaves to be covered in a white powdery mildew. Keeping the plant healthy and watered at the roots should help the plant to combat an attack. Also, there are varieties that are resistance to this fungus.

Botrytis

This is a fungus that causes a grey mold to form on soft fruit and plants such as strawberries and lettuce. Eventually it leads to the plant rotting and dying back. It is commonly found in greenhouses and cold frames or areas with poor air circulation. Remove infected material and improve ventilation.

Canker

There are both bacterial and fungal cankers that can affect most fruit trees. In stone fruit such as plums and cherries it causes orange gum to ooze from infected branches and the trunk. On apple trees it causes sunken and withered areas on the branch. Where possible, infected material should be removed and saws and pruners should be sterilized.

Club root

This is a fungal infection that affects members of the cabbage family, causing the root system to swell and distort, eventually resulting in the plant dying back. There are varieties that have resistance. Increasing the pH can help as it tends to be worse in acidic soil. Crop rotation can also help to reduce the problem, by moving the cabbages into soil where the fungus isn't present.

Damping off

This is a common fungal problem found on seedlings that causes them to underdevelop and then rot. It is usually found in the very early stages in a greenhouse. Remove infected material and improve the ventilation. Only water plants when the soil has just dried, as damp conditions cause the spread of this fungus.

Onion white rot

This fungus causes the browning and wilting of the foliage, eventually leading to the plant rotting and dying back. It affects onions, garlic, and leeks. The fungus can remain active in the ground for years, so replace the soil in a raised bed if the problem persists, or simply give in and grow a different crop.

Rust

There are a number of plants that can suffer from rust, which causes small orange pustules to appear on the leaves and stems. Infected material should be removed immediately to prevent it spreading. Crop rotation should help to reduce the problem, as should increasing air circulation and ensuring the plants receive plenty of sunlight.

Blight

This mainly affects potatoes and tomatoes. (They are from the same family). It causes the leaves to turn brown and die back, resulting in the loss of the plant. Tomato plants should be disposed of as soon as it is spotted. If caught in time, the foliage of potato plants can be cut back, which might prevent the potatoes themselves from becoming infected. Planting tomatoes in greenhouses can help to avoid the problem if you live in an area where it is a problem, as it gives them some protection from spores in the air.

WEEDS

It is often said that a weed is simply a plant growing in the wrong place. This is very true, and can range from anything from a tiny dandelion to a large ash tree seedling. If the plant isn't supposed to be there, then it is a weed. Gardeners should make every effort they can to keep their raised beds free of weeds. Within the bed there will be a limited amount of moisture and nutrients available for vegetables, fruit trees, and ornamental plants. Weeds, being the opportunists that they are, will compete and deprive them of this essential goodness. They will also spread outwards and upwards, reducing essential sunlight and space for your plants.

Annual weeds

Annual weeds are easier to eradicate than perennial weeds as they have a smaller root system. The trick is to catch them before they set seed and spread everywhere. The easiest way to eradicate them in large raised beds is to hoe them off. Choose a dry day and leave them to desiccate in the sun. If the weather is damp, then it is best to collect them up and add them to the compost. On smaller raised beds they can simply be removed by hand weeding among the plants. Alternatively, an onion hoe is a useful tool for pulling out annual weeds. The small handle and blade make it ideal for getting in amongst the plants without damaging them.

Prevention is better than cure, and time spent stopping weeds from establishing in the first place will save hours of weeding later. Consider covering up any bare soil with weed-suppressing cloth to prevent weed seed blowing onto the exposed area and germinating. Some gardeners like to use a weed-suppressing cloth permanently and cut holes through it to plant into. This is an effective method of controlling weeds long term, but can create difficulties with annual vegetable beds where the ground needs to be dug over each year and organic matter added.

COMMON TYPES OF ANNUAL WEEDS

CRABGRASS
ANNUAL NETTLE
SMARTWEED
PIGWEED
CHICKWEED
PURSLANE
LAMB'S QUARTER

Another method of controlling annual weeds is to use a natural mulch such as garden compost or rotted horse manure on the surface of the beds. This should help prevent the germination of weeds, but do be wary that some mulches can actually contain weed seed and could end up making the problem worse.

Perennial weeds

Perennial weeds can be very tricky to eradicate from raised beds once they have taken hold. The entire root system needs to be removed, otherwise it will keep regenerating. This is no easy task, as some roots can be deep down in the raised bed and entwined with the root systems of the plants you wish to keep. Taproots such as on dandelions can break easily when you try to remove them from the soil, which encourages them to regenerate, exacerbating the problem. Avoid adding fresh perennial weed roots to your compost heap, as they will quickly grow and regenerate in it.

In really severe cases, it may be best to empty the raised bed that is infested with perennial weed roots and fill it with fresh soil and compost. Do be aware that perennial roots could also be in the wood or brick cracks and joints, so use a knife to run around the edges of the raised bed to check that no roots remain. Lining the sides and floor of the beds with weed-suppressing cloth should prevent perennial roots from invading from outside.

If you use chemicals, then spraying or wiping foliage with a systemic weedkiller containing glyphosate should help kill the plant at the roots. However, be very careful not to let any of the chemical come into contact with the plants you wish to keep as you will end up losing them too. A trick to enable bindweed to be sprayed without harming other plants is to wind it around bamboo canes, which keeps it off the other plants, before spraying it a few days later.

WEEDS FOR WILDLIFE

If you have room in your garden, away from the raised beds, it is worth leaving a few weeds as they can be beneficial to wildlife. Do be wary of them seeding or spreading their roots further into your garden, though.

COMMON TYPES OF PERENNIAL WEEDS

PERENNIAL NETTLE

NUTSEDGE

CANADA THISTLE

BINDWEED

RAGWORT (ALTHOUGH TECHNICALLY A BIENNIAL)

DANDELION

CREEPING CHARLIE

BRAMBLE

PLANTAIN

JAPANESE KNOTWEED

CROP ROTATION

If you are planning on growing vegetables, it is worth considering having three or four individual raised beds or subdividing larger beds into sections. This will help you to manage your crops and enable them to be rotated each year.

Why rotate?

Crop rotation is a popular system among gardeners where specific groups of vegetables are grown in different beds each year. There are a variety of reasons for this, the main one being that it prevents a build-up of pests and diseases in the soil. Many are specific to a certain type of vegetable, so the theory is that by planting different types of crop in the soil each year it will prevent any problems from getting worse.

In addition, vegetables have different nutrient requirements, so growing them in different beds each year help to avoid a complete depletion of goodness in the soil. In fact, some vegetables will even gain nutrients by following another group of plants. For example, legumes (members of the pea family) fix nitrogen in the soil, meaning that the vegetables planted in the soil the following season will benefit from this extra boost of natural fertilizer.

Year 1
Roots and potatoes—ideal for breaking up soil

THREE-YEAR PLAN

Year 3
Cabbages require rich soil left by pea family

Year 2
Legumes and peas benefit from deep root run left by root family

Do note that crop rotation is only for annual crops. Perennial fruit and vegetables such as rhubarb, strawberries, globe and Jerusalem artichokes, and asparagus are not included in the system. However, after a few years, they will also benefit from being replanted in new beds so that they can take advantage of fresh soil and avoid pest and disease problems.

Most gardeners rotate crops over a three-year plan with the following categories:

- Root crops
- Legumes
- Brassicas

Note that brassicas and other leafy crops usually follow the legumes, which fix the nitrogen that the brassicas use.

EXTENDING THE SEASON

For centuries gardeners have attempted to grow fruits and vegetables for as long a season as possible. This could include forcing strawberries so they appear on the table in mid spring rather than early summer, or harvesting carrots well into late autumn. Most of the techniques used to extend the season involve giving plants extra warmth and protection during the colder months. Growing crops in a raised bed will already cheat the seasons to some extent, as the soil will be slightly warmer than the ground. The improved drainage will also mean plants are less likely to sit in wet, cold soil during some of the colder months. However, there are other techniques that can also be used to get crops earlier in spring or later in autumn.

Cold frames

These are low frames designed to protect crops from the cold, which are usually used to "force" crops for an early start in the year. They usually have a glass or PVC top to allow sunlight to penetrate into the frame, often hinged to enable them to be vented on particularly warm days. The sides are usually constructed from brick or timber. Crops can be planted in them and the extra warmth provided by the structure will provide vegetables a few weeks earlier than if they were grown directly outdoors. Gardeners also use them to "harden off" young seedlings. Young plants that have been grown in the comfy warmth of a greenhouse or on a window ledge in a centrally heated house will go into shock if planted directly into the cold spring soil. Cold frames can act as halfway houses to toughen up the plants, exposing them to a moderate amount of coolness, before planting them directly outside.

Cloches

These are transparent glass or plastic structures that can be placed over plants in raised beds to protect them from the frost and provide extra warmth for an earlier crop in spring or extend the season into autumn. Originally they were called cloches after the French word for bell due to their shape. However, gardening cloches these days include low tunnels made of glass or polythene that can be placed over rows of vegetables.

Greenhouses

If a garden has space, then a greenhouse is perfect for providing extra warmth and shelter for early or later crops. Raised beds can be built inside the greenhouse for ease of maintenance.

MAINTENANCE THROUGHOUT THE YEAR

There are a few essential jobs that you need to do throughout the year to ensure your raised beds are looking in tip-top form. Little and often is the best way to stay on top of the maintenance of the garden. Surprisingly, even in winter, when most plants are dormant and most of the vegetable beds lie empty, there are still plenty of garden tasks to take care of. Follow the seasonal guide on pages 62–63 to stay on top of gardening tasks throughout the year.

Staking plants

Many ornamental plants will require staking in early spring to prevent them flopping over the edges of the raised beds and onto the paths. The trick with staking to make it look natural is to get it in place before it is too late. It is best to allow the plant to grow through the staking structure rather than trying to get the plant upright once it has started to flop over. In the latter case it can look contrived, unnatural, and artificially trussed up. Staking materials include the following:

- Brush, such as from birch or willows, can be used to create an attractive rustic structure among the raised bed.

- Chain link stakes can be bought online or from a garden center. They are usually plastic or metal and link together to go around the plants.

- Single stakes are often used to support young trees and fruit bushes.

- Netting can be stretched tightly between posts to allow plants to scramble through them.

- Small sticks or twigs are ideal for allowing peas and some bean varieties to scramble through them.

- Willow teepees can be used to train up sweet peas or French and runner beans.

DEADHEADING

Once flowers have started to fade, they should be removed to encourage the plant to channel its energy into producing new flowers. Roses and sweet peas react particularly well to this and can go on producing amazing floral displays for months if regularly deadheaded.

Little and often is the best way to stay on top of the maintenance of the garden.

WINTER

☑ Check the structure of the raised beds. Wooden sections could have started to rot away, whereas brick beds may need repointing. As more material is added to the beds, it may be necessary to add another level or tier to the depth of the raised bed.

☑ Consider changing over the compost or soil in small raised beds every few years. This should help to avoid the build-up of pests and diseases. Alternatively, operate a crop rotation policy (see pages 56–57).

☑ Order vegetable seeds to grow in your raised beds for the next growing season.

☑ While the plants aren't growing, now is a good time to build more raised beds, construct paths and consider creating compost heaps.

☑ Prune fruit trees and bushes.

☑ Plant fruit and ornamental trees and shrubs in raised beds.

☑ Dig over any empty raised beds and rake them level.

SUMMER

☑ Deadhead plants to ensure plants keep flowering.

☑ Tie in climbing and scrambling plants to their training structures to keep them neat and tidy.

☑ Cut back some of your herbaceous perennial plants to near ground level in early summer (done too late and the plants may never flower). This extends the flowering season. It works really well on raised beds as they flower at a lower height, making them more contained and restrained in restricted spaces.

☑ Keep on top of the weeding. Hoe out annual weeds and dig out perennial weeds, ensuring all the roots are removed.

☑ Check plants to make sure they're not drying out and water them when needed.

☑ Start to pick and harvest crops in the vegetable garden.

SPRING

☑ Mulch the surfaces of the raised bed to help retain moisture and suppress weeds. If you mulch in winter, then all the goodness may have washed through by the time you need it.

☑ Put climbing structures and staking in place early on in the season.

☑ Keep a vigilant eye out for pests and diseases. Try to catch any problems before it's too late.

☑ Divide herbaceous plants and replant them in other areas of the raised beds.

☑ Sow vegetable seeds as soon as the season has warmed up enough.

AUTUMN

☑ Autumn is a good time to plant trees and shrubs as the soil is warm and roots should establish easily.

☑ Cover over vegetables with a frost cloth or cloches to try and extend the season. Move tender plants into a greenhouse if you have one.

☑ Continue to harvest crops from the vegetable garden and store them appropriately—for example by preserving, pickling, or freezing them—so that you have a supply of fresh ingredients during winter.

☑ Clear fallen leaves off the raised bed, collect them up, and add them to the compost.

☑ Install a rain barrel and attach guttering to sheds and outside structures in anticipation of catching the rain over the winter period.

Part 2:
TYPES OF RAISED BEDS

There are all sorts of raised beds to suit everybody's space, taste, and budget. For those with no budget at all, it is possible to construct raised beds purely from recycled material that can be found for free. Other types may cost a bit, but you will find the resulting raised beds will transform your garden, and give you many years of gardening enjoyment as they provide you with space to grow your own vegetables or cut flowers for the cost of a few packets of seeds.

READY-MADE RAISED BEDS

Nothing could be simpler than a ready-made raised bed. Simply unpack it, fill it with soil, and get planting or sowing. There are a few different designs available, so pick those that are a comfortable height for you to work at, will provide you with enough growing space, and fit in with the style of your existing garden.

Pre-made metal raised beds

If you love the retro look in your garden, pre-fabricated metal raised beds could be ideal. They're usually made from Aluzinc steel panels, with stainless steel fasteners and stabilized safety edging. They come in various shapes and sizes and are ideal for growing annual vegetables and cut flowers. They make a beautiful feature outside the kitchen door, on the patio, or even on a balcony.

Wooden raised bed tables

Raised tables are useful if you want to raise the height of your growing crops, but don't want to have to fill up the entire depth of a raised bed with soil. They are ideal for short-term annual crops with shallow root runs such as head lettuce, cut-and-come-again, and other salad crops. They're also ideal for growing strawberries, allowing their trails to hang over the sides, and keeping them away from slugs and snails. They suit small gardens, patio and courtyard gardens and balconies. They are very easy to maintain and are the perfect height to work comfortably at without bending over and straining your back. Popular sizes on the market are 2 feet by 4 feet or 4 feet by 4 feet. They usually come 1 or 2 feet deep. Most tables also come with a thick non-woven polypropylene fabric liner to aid water retention and help preserve the longevity of the timber.

Raised troughs

Similar to raised wooden tables, raised troughs (sometimes called mangers) provide a comfortable height for growing all your vegetables, herbs, and strawberries in. They come in a range of different sizes, but the one advantage troughs have over tables is the additional depth in the center of the bed. It means that deeper-rooted plants such as carrots and parsnips can be planted where there could be as much as 2 feet depth of soil. The outside edges of the trough, where it is not so deep, can then be planted with shallower rooting vegetables. There should be a liner in the base and sides of the inside of the trough to help with water retention and to protect the wood from deteriorating. Most pre-built troughs will come with a guarantee, usually for three years. Troughs are perfect for squeezing into small gardens, courtyards, and balconies. Place it close to the kitchen door, making it quick and easy to pop out and harvest salad crops and herbs.

SELF-ASSEMBLY KITS

Everybody appreciates something that makes life simpler, and self-assembly raised bed kits do exactly that. They come in all shapes and sizes to suit personal budgets, but there are a few things to consider before taking the plunge and buying one.

Self-assembly kit checklist

☑ **Does the style fit in with the existing design of the garden?**
If you already have raised beds, then the new one should be of a similar style and made of the same material, or at the very least not clash with the current ones.

☑ **How durable is it?**
You don't want to spend lots of money on a raised bed, only for it to break apart after a season of use. Some come with three-year structural guarantees; it's worth checking before purchasing.

☑ **How easy is it to assemble?**
Some kits are very simple to put together, some are more complicated, and you may find that at the end of the day, it would have been easier to have knocked one together yourself with some recycled lumber. Many gardening and lifestyle websites have customer reviews of raised bed kits, so don't forget to check these out before purchasing.

☑ **Will it fit?**
It may sound obvious, but make sure that when you purchase a raised bed kit, you are leaving plenty of space around it for access. Ideally you should be able to access the bed from all sides to avoid walking across the beds.

☑ **Any extras with that?**
Many come with optional extras such as cappings that run along the top to give an elegant finish, or attachable features such as seating benches, or even compost heaps. Don't forget to take these into account before buying.

Wooden board raised bed kits

The most popular type of raised bed to be bought in kit form for self-assembly is the standard wooden board type. They offer good value for money and can come in most lengths and widths, giving a good degree of flexibility in the garden.

Boards are usually about 6 inches deep, but better quality ones can be 8 inches deep. They are often up to five or six tiers tall. Five 6 inch-deep boards provide a 2.5 foot-tall bed, which is the most comfortable height for wheelchair users to garden at. Lumber varies in quality but it is often Scandinavian softwood that has been high-pressure treated with a non-toxic preservative. The boards are usually between ¾ and 1.5 inches thick (depending on quality) to provide a sturdy structure capable of retaining the weight of the soil.

One of the benefits of purchasing a wooden board raised bed kit is that there are usually fitted covers and hoops available that fit perfectly over the plants to protect them from either frost or pests.

What's included?

Wooden board kits are likely to come with all or some of the following. Check what's included before you buy.

- ☑ Full instructions on how to build the bed.

- ☑ Pre-drilled planks.

- ☑ Internal wooden corner fixing posts or aluminium fixing brackets.

- ☑ Galvanized or stainless steel screws.

- ☑ Stout wooden posts for the corners (which give the bed a chunky look).

- ☑ Cappings (for an attractive finish).

- ☑ Two- or three-year structural guarantee, depending on the quality of the wood (e.g. ¾ inches thick, two years/1.5 inches thick, three years).

CORNER RAISED BEDS

Wooden kits often also offer a corner option, which is perfect for people with a small garden. They can fit into the tiniest of spaces, maximizing the number of vegetables that can be grown in the back garden. Again, they usually come in a range of sizes, including different heights to suit personal requirements.

Modular self-assembly kits

There is a range of modular self-assembly kits available on the market. They come with all the relevant parts for assembly included, are easy to assemble and can be made into whatever size you please. Here are just three of the popular options available in the US:

- **Greenland Gardener**: These raised bed kits require no tools to assemble. They can be put together in minutes by even the least handy people! They're made from composite lumber that incorporates recycled materials. You simply knock the side pieces into the corner pieces, fill with soil, and you're ready to plant! They are not very deep, though, so you'll want to stack two on top of each other to grow root crops.

- **Greenes Fence:** These raised beds give you a more upscale look. They are usually made from cedar and come in a variety of different configurations, including double beds side by side, a step-like tier system that allows you to grow shallow-rooted crops in the front and root crops in the back. They require more tools and time to assemble, but offer elegance and affordability.

- **Gardener's Supply:** If you're going for a more modern, sleek design but still want wood, take a look at the cedar beds from Gardener's Supply. They come with minimalistic metal corner pieces that make assembly easy. Gardener's also has many other types of raised bed kits available, including the manger-style and metal trough-style beds.

HUGELKULTUR

This northern European horticultural philosophy is increasing in popularity as people look for self-sustaining methods of gardening that reduce the need for watering and feeding plants. The system relies on the decomposition of wood. This process provides an environment that acts like a sponge, holding and releasing moisture and nutrients when required. It also generates a moderate amount of heat, providing warmer growing conditions and thereby early crops.

What is hugelkultur?

Hugelkultur means hill culture and it involves mounding up rotting logs, branches, and sticks into piles and covering them with soil so they look like mini hills. Crops are then planted onto the sides and tops of them. It has been suggested that the retention of moisture and nutrients is so good in hugelkultur that they could be created in deserts and the plants would thrive purely from the goodness in the hugel bed. The beds can be as big or small as you like. In some places, entire tree trunks are buried and left to decompose in the ground. In small urban places, small mounds can be created with just bundles of sticks.

Simplicity

One of the biggest advantages of this style of raised bed is that all the material should be free, as it should be possible to source it locally from recycled materials. It also requires practically no DIY skills. There is no bolting or screwing of beds together; it simply involves using a spade to bury the logs with soil or compost.

Steepness

Some hugel-gardeners make their beds with very steep sides, about 45 degrees and to a height of up to 6 feet. The advantages are that the crops growing on the sides are at a comfortable height for harvesting and it provides a larger area of planting for vegetables than a flatter bed. It also reduces long-term compaction, but be aware that it creates additional shade on the north and east sides.

It has been suggested that the retention of moisture and nutrients is so good in hugelkultur that they could be created in deserts and the plants would thrive.

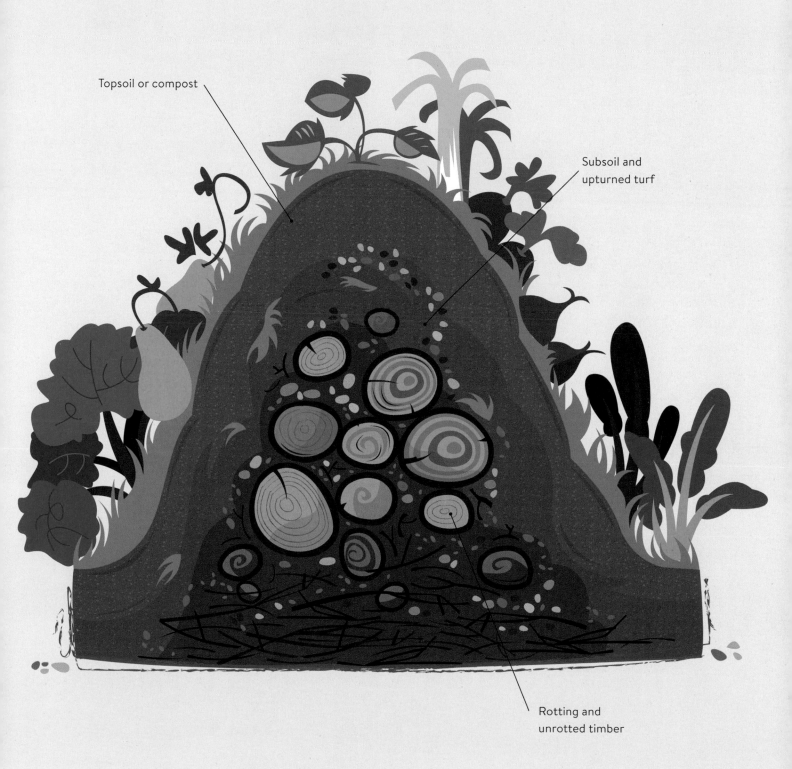

Topsoil or compost

Subsoil and
upturned turf

Rotting and
unrotted timber

How to build a hugelkultur bed

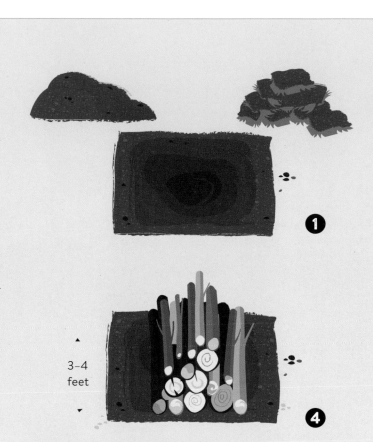

1 | *Remove the turf from the area where you intend to place the hugel beds. Save the sod pieces for later.*

2 | *Dig out the remaining soil to a depth of about 12 inches. Save the soil for later. If there is a clear difference between the topsoil and subsoil, then keep them separate too.*

3 | *Stack logs and timber in the pit, with the largest at the bottom. Use both rotting and unrotted timber. The more timber you include in your bed, the more nutrients and water it will provide and the longer it will last.*

4 | *Build up the height of wood to about 3-4 feet above ground level, depending on the height you wish to have your raised bed at.*

3–4 feet

5 | *Cover over the logs with layers of upturned turf and the subsoil. Push some of the soil between the gaps in the timber to get the rotting process going.*

6 | *Cover the sides and the top with topsoil or compost. Sculpt and rake the soil so that it is shaped like a mound.*

7 | *You are now ready for planting. Most people plant annual vegetable crops, but hugel beds can also be used for perennials, shrubs, and trees.*

8 | *The edges of the beds can be finished off with lengths of lumber if necessary. This gives the bed some definition and may prevent surrounding weeds creeping onto the hugel bed.*

MAINTENANCE

There is very little to the maintenance of a hugel bed because they are so self-sufficient. After a while, the structure may start to sag as the timber begins to rot, so it may be necessary to add more soil and re-contour the slopes. Young plants, particularly in the first year or so, will need additional watering to get them established as the benefits of the rotting timber may not occur immediately. Regularly check on any weeds and be ready to remove perennial weeds before they have a chance to get established. Apart from that, there is very little to it.

As a general rule, hugel beds shouldn't be dug over like a traditional vegetable bed as they rely on the natural soil structure occurring in the rotting timber below. Obviously some addition of soil may be necessary to remove weeds and for planting, but it should be kept to a minimum, with compost and green and brown material being added to the surface of the bed, allowing the worms and the rain to take it down to the root system.

Which wood?

Large, single unrotted lengths of timber will take the longest amount of time to break down and so will provide the best longevity for a raised bed, but also take a while before their decomposition benefits the plant. At the other extreme, wood chips will break down very quickly, but only provide two or three years of nutrients, moisture and heat. A mix of both is a good compromise. Make sure there is plenty of soil between the rotting timber and the root area of the vegetable plants, because the rotting process can deplete the soil of nitrogen.

KEYHOLE GARDENS

Keyhole gardening originated in Africa, but its popularity has spread worldwide. It is an ingenious concept that is based on a circular raised bed with a notch cut out of it for ease of access and maintenance. From an aerial view it has the shape of a keyhole, hence the name. At the very center of the bed is a compost bin which is accessed via the notch. This gradually leaches out its goodness into the surrounding soil, providing it with nutrients and moisture. It is, in effect, a self-sustaining raised bed system. Due to the extra rich and deep soil it means plants can be planted closer together than if they were grown in the ground. The principle can be adapted to any type of raised bed situation. It is not absolutely necessary that the bed is circular: you can experiment with shape.

In the frame

Because of the compact size of the raised bed it means frameworks can be created over the beds using wires. During the summer it can be used to train climbing plants such as runner and French beans or sweet peas. They can also be used to support shade netting or cloths during very hot weather. In early spring or late autumn plastic sheeting can be pulled over it to act like a mini polytunnel, protecting crops from frosts and the extreme cold.

Bed-building materials

Traditionally in Africa, rocks and stones were used to create the outside walls as they were in numerous supply. One of the key principles to keyhole gardening is recycling, and being encouraged to use whatever free material is available. An additional benefit of rocks is that they absorb warmth during the day, making the soil warmer during the night, which gives faster growth rates for the crops. Other materials that can be used include corrugated metal, and bricks either laid on their sides in a herringbone pattern or cemented like a wall. Lumber can be used, but it is harder to create a curve with it. One recycling idea is to fill large plastic milk bottles with soil and use them as the building blocks to create the keyhole garden. You are limited only by your imagination: try old glass bottles, old drainpipes, empty paint pots… whatever you have to hand.

What to fill your keyhole bed with

The keyhole philosophy of gardening depends very much on having moisture-retentive soil that will provide a gradual release of nutrients. It shouldn't be too fast draining or too heavy. Filling the bed with layers of different types of material helps to provide this growing medium. Materials could include wood and wood chips on the bottom layer; cardboard; manure and compost; newspaper; manure and compost; wood ash; straw; manure and compost; topsoil.

MAINTENANCE

Keyhole raised beds are easy to maintain as they are practically self-supporting. Crops will need less watering than in conventional raised beds, though do keep an eye out for wilting plants during hot weather. Occasionally water the compost bin; the moisture will in turn leach out into the plants. However, plants may need additional watering. This will particularly be the case towards the outside of the beds as these are farthest from the compost heap and therefore are more prone to drying out and suffering due to lack of nutrients.

Due to the improved fertility and nutrient content of the soil, thanks to the central composting system, there will also be lots of weeds germinating. Dig them out as soon as you spot them. Annual weeds can simply be added back into the compost bin, but perennial weeds should be disposed of elsewhere.

Regularly keep the compost bin topped off with kitchen green waste, grass clippings, newspaper, and so forth. If the bin stops getting "fed," the entire process comes to a halt. In Africa the compost bins are often given roofs (usually thatched from straw) to keep the compost warm, to stop them from drying out, and to speed up the process of decomposition.

How to make a keyhole garden

1 | *Clear a space for the keyhole garden. Not only will you need space for the actual keyhole garden, but you will also need space around it for access. Remove any perennial weeds. The ideal diameter for a keyhole garden is 10 feet, as it allows you to reach all parts of the bed without standing on it. However, keyhole beds can be whatever size suits your area of garden. Traditionally they are round, but you could experiment with the shape should you wish.*

2 | *Place a bamboo cane in the center of where the raised bed will be, tie string to it and attach another bamboo cane to the other end of the string at 5 feet wide. Use this guide to scratch out the outline of the 10 foot circular raised bed.*

3 | *Mark out a notch in the circle, approximately one-eighth of the total area. This notch will allow you access to the compost bin at the center.*

4 | *Use a fork to dig over the soil to break up any compaction. Next, start to build up the exterior wall. Almost any durable material can be used, although the traditional material is rocks. The ideal height of the wall is about 3 feet, but this can be varied to suit individual needs.*

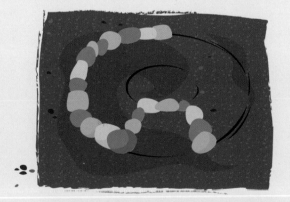

5 | *Now construct the compost bin for the center of the bed. Traditionally this is created by weaving together flexible sticks or canes. Willow or bamboo would be suitable. Far easier, though, is to create a tube using chicken wire or wire mesh with a diameter of about 2 feet and about 4 feet high. Secure it in place using bamboo canes pushed through the mesh.*

6 | *Line the insides of the outer walls of the raised bed with cardboard or straw and then add layers of biodegradable material, wetting it down as you go. Fill the last few inches with weed-free topsoil. The soil should slope down from near the top of the basket to the outside wall to encourage water and moisture towards the outer edges.*

7 | *Add alternating layers of brown and green waste materials such as cardboard and kitchen scraps to the compost bin. These provide the plants with moisture and nutrients. Don't quite fill it—leave room to add new material.*

8 | *Your keyhole garden is now ready to plant. Water the newly planted seedlings or any seeds that are sown. However, try to avoid regularly watering the plants. Infrequent watering forces the roots down towards the center of the bed, making them self-sustaining. Ideal if you are planning on going on vacation for a week or two!*

❺

❼

TURF RAISED BEDS

For a completely natural and green raised bed, nothing could be simpler than creating one out of grass turf. Not only does it look great, it is easy to make, requiring practically no DIY skills. If you are removing turf from a section of your garden, for example, to create a path or patio, then the material for the raised bed is completely free, too. Turf (sod) squares provide a solid structure and are the building blocks for the bed. Being of completely natural material, they will encourage wildlife into the garden. Due to the soft material of turf, the edges of the raised bed make a comfy seat, too.

MAINTENANCE

Turf beds are relatively maintenance free. They should last for years, although they will gradually sink as the soil gradually decomposes and erodes. However, simply by adding fresh turf to the top layer, you can retain the height of the raised bed.

If you want to keep the grass cut, then it is best to use a string trimmer every few weeks during the growing season. Occasionally you may want to pull out any perennial weeds such as dandelions and daisies from the turf walls, although you may be just as happy to retain them as an extra splash of color.

Turfing iron

A turfing iron is a tool used by landscapers to lift turf from a lawn. It has a spade-shaped head but is pointed to help cut through the grass. The long handle has a curve in it, which is cleverly designed to keep the back of the spade flush with the ground, helping you cut turf squares to the same depth each time.

How to make a turf raised bed

1 | You can buy turf sod pieces from a sod farm or garden center but it is much better to recycle slices of turf from an area of your garden. Use a half moon (a garden tool used to cut through turf) to cut down through the turf, creating rectangular shapes that are about 12 inches by 20 inches. Then use a turfing iron or spade to cut horizontally through the roots to a depth of about 1.5 inches to leave you with slices of turf. These will be the building blocks of your raised bed.

2 | Mark out where the raised bed is going to be built using string or sand. Don't forget that if you're building the raised bed on an existing lawn, then the turf below can be removed and used to create the walls too.

3 | Start to lay the sod pieces along the proposed outline of the raised bed, placing them with the grass side facing downwards. Build up the layers to the desired height. The structure will be stronger if you stagger the sod pieces, like brickwork. Use wooden pegs or stakes and bang them through the center of the turf wall every meter to help keep the sod in place.

4 | For the final layer, first place a 1 inch layer of topsoil. The sod should be placed on the topsoil, but this time with the grass facing upwards. Firm the turf down so that it beds into the topsoil below.

5 | When it is all done, the sod should be watered to keep the top lush and green. If the raised bed has been built in the summer, it will need watering most days during dry periods for the first few weeks until it is established.

6 | If you wish and you have spare turf, you can use wire pegs to pin additional grass strips to the sides of the bed. For a final flourish, if you don't intend to use the top as turf seats, you could sow a wild flower mix into the sod for an additional splash of color and to attract more wildlife.

7 | The turf raised bed is now ready for use. It can be filled with topsoil and compost and planted.

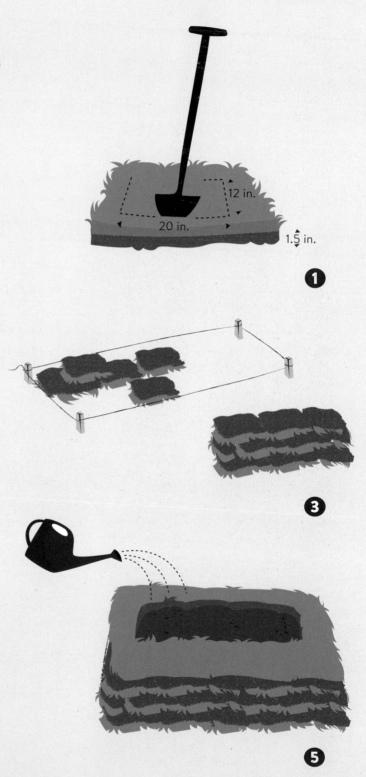

WOVEN RAISED BEDS

This type of raised bed is ideal for a cottage garden and an attractive feature in its own right. Using supple branches to create structures is one of the oldest forms of construction. Many medieval buildings were built using a technique of wattle and daub, based on weaving branches (wattle) to create the structure. It was revived during the Arts and Crafts Movement of the early twentieth century, and recently there has once again been a resurgence of this traditional, rustic technique in the garden.

Flexible edges

The beauty of using flexible willow branches is that you can create curvy sides just as easily as straight edges on the raised bed. So you can be as imaginative as you like in terms of shape. In fact, it would be a lovely type of wall for a keyhole garden (see pages 76–79).

Using supple branches to create structures is one of the oldest forms of construction.

How to make a woven raised bed in your garden

1 | *Clear the area where the raised bed is going to be constructed and mark out the shape of it on the ground using sand or string.*

2 | *Use a sledge hammer to tap thick wooden stakes into the ground where the corners are going to be. In addition, also place sturdy hazel stakes every 20 inches or so along the sides. Willow can be used, but oak and chestnut are just as good. Briefly charring them over a fire will harden the wood and should make them last longer in the soil.*

3 | *Take lengths of young willow branches and weave them between the posts, passing each branch in front of one post and then behind the next. When starting the next row, place the branch on the opposite side of the post to where the one below it started.*

4 | *As the willow is worked around the raised bed structure, it is important to keep pushing down on it to keep it as tight as possible. Stop once the raised bed is at the desired height.*

5 | *Due to the fast perishing nature of the woven-bed structures, it is worth lining the inside with a horticultural fabric liner or black plastic sheeting before filling the bed with soil and compost. This should increase the willow branches' life by a few more years.*

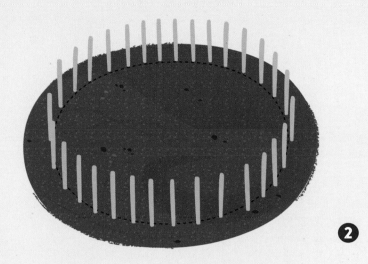

2

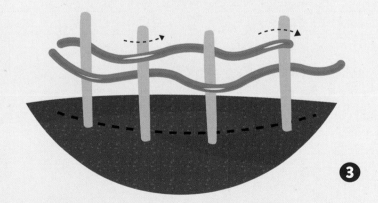

3

Taking it further

If you actually want to create an authentic wattle and daub raised bed, then you are going to have to get a bit dirty. The woven part is referred to as the wattle; the muddy material that makes it watertight is the daub. The four essential ingredients are straw, soil, cow manure, and water. Mix the first three ingredients together in equal proportions on a wooden board and then add the water—traditionally, this would have been mixed by the craftsman's feet, or by livestock for large structures. Using your spade to thoroughly mix up the daub should suffice here to make it a thick but flexible material. The daub is picked up by hand and "splattered" or thrown onto the woven structure, starting at the bottom. The palm is then used to smooth it out, pushing it into all the cracks. The daub should be about an inch and a half thick. Finally, go and take a shower!

MAINTENANCE

The woven material should last for two or three years and will then need replacing. The posts should last for a few years longer. To replace the material, simply remove the branches and repeat the process with newer, flexible branches. The older branches can be shredded or chipped and then added to the surface of the soil to act as a mulch, which will help to retain the moisture and suppress weeds.

RECYCLED PALLET RAISED BEDS

Pallets are a recycler's best friend. The wood is strong and durable and pallets can usually be found going for free outside most warehouses or around the back of retail shops. Do always ask the permission of the owners, though, as sometimes pallets need to be returned to the depots they came from. Although they might look a bit rough and ready, with a bit of sanding and painting they can be transformed into a chic or funky raised bed that will be the envy of your neighbors. For the DIY enthusiast, accompanying tables, chairs, and benches can be made from pallets to complement the raised beds.

MAINTENANCE

Pallet raised beds should last for about five to ten years. The great news is that to replace them should cost nothing again, just a bit more of your time to make them. They may need repainting every couple of years, though. The soil or compost in the pallet raised bed will need to be regularly weeded and it may need topping off at the end of each year as the material gradually erodes and washes away.

Pallet raised beds should last for about five to ten years.

How to make a pallet raised bed

Construct this raised bed in the location it is going to remain in, because it will be heavy to move once built.

1 | *Select four pallets that are the same size to form the four sides of the bed. Having them the same size will make your job much easier because otherwise a lot of time will be taken up trying to make things fit. You might need to reduce the height of the pallets a bit so that they are the desired height for your raised bed. Remember to wear gloves when using a saw to do this.*

2 | *You will also need two or three extra pallets. Use a crowbar to remove slats from some of these pallets.*

3 | *Lay the four side pallets on the ground and screw the slats taken from the spare pallets over the gaps. This will prevent the soil spilling out of the sides.*

4 | *Stand the four sides upright and then screw metal corner brackets to the insides of the pallets to hold them together to form a box shape.*

5 | *Line the insides of the box with a landscape fabric or plastic sheeting to help prevent the sides from rotting.*

6 | *Attach more spare slats along the top edges to give it an attractive capped finish.*

7 | *Sand the box down and then paint it with a color of your choice, using an exterior undercoat first, followed by an exterior wood paint.*

8 | *Once the paint is dry, fill the box with compost and soil to just below the top and plant with vegetables or fruit trees. Water the plants in well.*

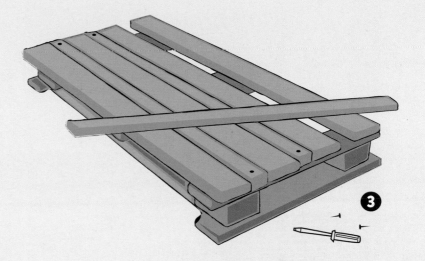

3

Corner bracket

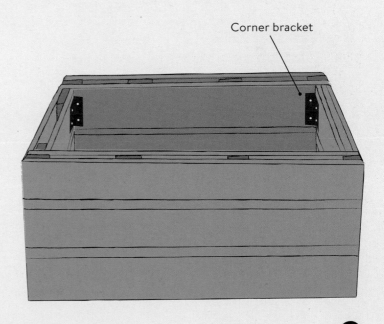

4

RECYCLED LUMBER RAISED BEDS

Creating a raised bed from recycled lumber requires a certain level of DIY skills as you have to work with the material you have salvaged. Planks won't always be the same width or depth, and so you will need a flexible and patient approach. However, with perseverance, you will end up with a custom, personalized raised bed that will have cost you absolutely nothing.

Sourcing lumber

Search in dumpsters (with the owner's permission) and you will often find pieces of wood that can be used. Always look for exterior wood and avoid materials that have come from inside houses such as furniture or wooden cabinets from the kitchen as they will quickly rot outside. Look for old bits of fencing, gravel boards, wooden posts; even sections of sheds can be cut up and used as walls for a raised bed. Raised beds can be made simply from the offcuts of posts, or logs upturned in the ground.

Be creative

Lumber can be painted to personalize it and give it a distinctive style. Always use an undercoat first, followed by a wood paint, or use a wood stain. Painting your recycled lumber with soft pastel and cream colors will give your garden a calm, muted yet sophisticated feel, whereas bright oranges, reds, and pinks will make a bold statement, making the raised bed a feature in its own right. Be creative: try covering it with colorful graffiti writing for an urban, city feel, or personalize it to fit in with a theme; for example, alternate black and yellow painted panels on your raised bed if you're going to keep a beehive on it.

MAINTENANCE

Depending on the type of wood used, the lumber in a recycled lumber bed should last between five and ten years. Softwood will not last as long as hardwood. The soil or compost will gradually break down and leach out, so it will usually need topping off with fresh material at the end of the year. If there are perennial plants in the bed, they will need digging out in late autumn or early summer in order to top off with soil, before replanting them.

How to make a raised bed from recycled lumber

1 | *Use strings to mark out the shape of the raised bed. The bed can be whatever size you like, but no wider than 4-6 feet is ideal because it means you can stretch 2-3 feet across to reach the center of the bed without walking on the soil.*

2 | *Following the shape, dig out trenches that are half the depth of the posts that are being used. This is deeper than you would put posts in usually, but because these will only be supported by soil without any bracing this extra depth is important.*

3 | *Bang the posts into the ground using a rubber mallet, ensuring they are upright.*

4 | *Cut the four sides for your raised bed from the recycled lumber with a saw (remember to wear gloves). Screw them to the outside of the posts to create the first tiers.*

5 | *Continue to add the tiers, screwing them to the posts as you go. Finally, cut the posts flush to the top of the raised bed to make them look neat. Alternatively, you can leave the posts uncut so that they can be used as a framework for nets and frost cloth to be draped over.*

Don't make your recycled lumber raised bed any taller than 20 inches because otherwise it will need bracing and structures to hold the posts together. This style is sometimes called palisade.

RAISED BEDS FROM OTHER RECYCLED MATERIALS

One person's trash can be another person's treasure. Almost anything can be used to create a raised bed and much of it can be found for free. Not only does using recycled materials to make a raised bed make good sense environmentally, it is also very fashionable. Whether you want to create something that looks bohemian or shabby chic, using recycled material creatively and artistically can leave your neighbors thinking you employed top garden designers.

Trash cans

Old plastic and metal trash cans are ideal for making into raised beds. Three or four drainage holes should be drilled in the bottom, and then the cans filled up to just below the rim with compost. If you're only planning on growing annual crops, then the bottom half can be filled with polystyrene or rubbish to save on the cost of compost. They also make good containers for fruit trees. Single-specimen edible plants with architectural foliage, such as globe artichokes or rhubarb, also look great. Wheelie bins can be converted into raised beds in the same way.

Bathtubs

Builders are often ripping out old tin or metal/enamel bathtubs and replacing them with new ones. Contact local builders and they will usually be more than happy for you to take them off their hands. Simply top them up with soil and plant them up. Very usefully, they already have drainage provided by the plug hole, but you may want to drill a few more holes if you don't think this will be enough.

Wheelbarrows

There's no need to consign an old barrow to the trash just because it is old and rusty, or has sprung a few punctures. It makes an attractive mini raised bed and can be moved easily around the garden to whichever position suits you. All you need to do is punch a few drainage holes in the base and then fill to just below the brim with a good quality general-purpose compost.

Scrap cars and boats

Raised beds can even be made from old scrap vehicles. Fill their trunks, hoods, or the inside bodies on old convertibles with compost and plant out veggies, herbs, or cut flowers. The inside of a car (supposing the windshield and windows are still in place) makes a good mini greenhouse, especially if the car has a sunroof! Around seaside areas you will often see old fishing boats in front gardens and public parks that have been filled with soil and planted with annual bedding displays.

Glass bottles and jars

Wine bottles can be used to create an artistic looking raised bed. Fill the bottles up with sand (to make them more weighty and sturdy, and less prone to break) and dig them neck first into the soil in a row to form a low retaining wall. Beer and other drink cans can be used in a similar way.

Maintenance

Recycled material can last for years. When it finally deteriorates, it shouldn't cost you anything to replace like with like. As with all raised beds, they will need topping off with soil every one or two years as the material gradually leaches away. Keep an eye on raised beds made from metal, such as bins or bathtubs, as they will heat up quickly in the summer, which can cause the soil to dry out near the edges; plants near these areas will need extra watering.

BULK BAGS

Large woven builder's bags make fantastic instant raised beds that can be placed anywhere in the garden as a feature. Also called bulk bags, these are the large white bags that builders use to drop off material to domestic houses and building sites containing material such as topsoil, gravel, and compost. They usually have a 1-ton capacity, but there are other sizes. They may look a bit rough and ready, but it's wonderful to see freecycled materials adapted to be used in the garden. If you like, you could build a wooden frame around one, then clad with thinner bits of wood to make it look a bit smarter.

Why use bulk bags?

The bags are usually free. Ask at building sites or warehouses as they are usually more than happy to get rid of them. They are made of incredibly strong material and should last a good few years. When the bags are full, they're at a perfect height for working. They have good depth to them once filled with soil or compost, meaning that deep-rooted vegetables such as carrots, parsnips and leeks can be grown in them. They're flexible in that they can be moved into a different position after a cropping; simply empty the soil before relocating them. The material is porous so excess water will naturally drain off—you won't need to worry about drainage holes at the bottom.

What to plant in them

You may as well take advantage of the deep soil. Plants from the cucurbit family will do well, as long as there is lots of rich compost in there. Consider growing pumpkins or squashes. A couple in the top should suffice. Their trails can then hang down the side, disguising the woven fabric of the bulk bag. Alternatively, eight tomato plants can be planted around the edges, trained up on a system of stakes, making them easy to harvest.

Siting your bulk bag

Think carefully about where you are going to position your bulk bag before filling it with compost, because a 1-ton bag is very hard to move once you've planted it. In order to reduce the amount of compost needed to fill the bag and make it lighter, you could half fill it with bits of polystyrene left over from packaging. Cover this with plastic sheeting before topping off with compost, so that the compost doesn't fall down between the pieces of polystyrene. Ideally the bag should be in maximum sunlight, meaning you can grow a greater range of plants.

MAINTENANCE

Bulk bags will last for about three years before they need replacing. Each year they will need regular weeding. Bags should be topped off each year with fresh compost or soil. Bulk bags can be prone to drying out in warm weather, so check regularly to see if plants need watering.

Potatoes in compost bags

If you don't have room for a bulk bag then smaller bags can be used. Try using a 20 gallon compost bag to grow potatoes in. The sides of the compost bags can give some protection from the dreaded potato blight: rolling the bags up slightly higher than the stems reduces the chance of fungal spores landing directly on the plants. Potatoes should be planted in mid spring.

1 | *Cut small drainage holes in the compost bag, if there aren't some already.*

2 | *Roll the sides of the compost bag down to make it about 8 inches tall.*

3 | *Place about 4 inches of soil in the bottom of the bag.*

4 | *Place two potatoes on the compost with their "eyes" facing upwards.*

5 | *Cover over with about another 4 inches of soil.*

6 | *As the potato shoots grow the bag should be rolled up and topped off with compost, up to a height of 12-16 inches.*

7 | *Regularly water the potatoes, but don't overdo it because otherwise the tubers will rot.*

8 | *After the potato plants have flowered the bag can be ripped open and the potatoes harvested.*

STRAW BALE RAISED BEDS

Straw bales are the perfect building blocks for creating temporary raised beds. Aesthetically they may not suit every garden situation but they are ideal for small and larger gardens, particularly out in the countryside where straw bales are an easy commodity to come by.

Why straw bales?

As well as being easy to build, straw bale raised beds retain heat and provide excellent insulation for the crops growing in them. They also make excellent shelter from the wind if the crops are planted below the height of the walls, which is perfect for people gardening in large open spaces and exposed locations. And, of course, the wide structure of the bale provides the perfect soft seat. You can often get a few bales for relatively little money compared to bricks and lumber, although don't forget that they won't last as long.

How to build a straw bale raised bed

Building with straw bales couldn't be simpler.

1 | *Place the bales on the ground where you want them, usually in the shape of a square or rectangle.*

2 | *Secure them in place by driving wooden stakes through the center of them. You may not need to stake them if you are only creating one tier of bales, which is usually adequate for most people's requirements.*

3 | *Once the bales are in place they can be filled up with soil and compost, raked level, and then planted.*

4 | *Water the plants in thoroughly after planting.*

What to plant in them

You can plant fruit and vegetables directly into the bales. In fact, in some places such as school playgrounds or small urban gardens where there is just asphalt and concrete, this can be a very useful method of growing edible crops. Suitable crops include strawberries or tomatoes that are planted directly into the top of each bale. Pry open a hole with your hands that is about 4 inches by 4 inches and 6 inches deep. Fill it partly with compost, plant your fruit bush, and then backfill the remainder of the hole with compost and water the plant in thoroughly. You should be able to fit in three plants per bale. Pumpkins and squashes can also be planted into the bales, but restrict your planting to one per bale. Remember to keep the plants well watered and fed during the growing season and they should reward you with a bumper crop.

ROOFTOP GARDENS

Rooftop gardens must be the ultimate in raised beds. They are the perfect solution for urban living where there is a shortage of outdoor garden space. They add interest and color, attract wildlife such as pollinating bees and butterflies, and are a fantastic way of utilizing an unused area. In large cities you can see impressive gardens built on huge roofs that are open to the public. Some of them even support trees and their root systems, with large water features and 100 tons of material. Most people don't wish to create anything on this scale—just a place to sit, enjoy the view, and a few raised beds to grow some vegetables in.

A weighty question

If you want to construct a rooftop garden that you can actually walk onto, the first thing to consider is the weight load of the garden on the roof structure. This is something that should be calculated for you by a structural engineer. You will also need to consider building regulations if you intend to convert a window to a door to allow you access onto your flat roof. You may also need planning permission if you are planning on making structural changes to the roof and, of course, its "use," as it may affect surrounding neighbors' privacy and have a noise impact, particularly if the roof garden backs directly onto your neighbors' property.

No flat roof? No problem

If you don't have a flat space for a roof garden but are desperate to grow your own vegetables, then there may be other places. Outdoor staircases up to apartments can have containers laden with edible crops placed on them, so long as they aren't causing an obstruction for fire escapes. Trailing plants such as grapevines, beans and peas can be trained along the banisters. Finally, salad crops can be grown in window boxes. After all, every apartment or house has windows. The ideal location is the kitchen window, for ease of access to salad leaves or herbs. Just make sure that any window boxes are firmly secured.

Odd numbers

When selecting containers for your rooftop, select them in clusters of three or five. For some reason they look better than a group of even numbered containers. Also try to vary their heights slightly, with the taller ones towards the back.

How to create your rooftop garden

It is amazing how even the smallest house can accommodate a roof garden. The only criteria is a flat roof. These days so many houses have small extensions, usually at the back. If you're not intending to walk on it, but simply to place some pots or containers on it to admire from your sofa, then it couldn't be simpler.

1 | *Choose attractive looking containers that fit in with the style of your house. For a modern house, you could choose aluminum or a traditional terracotta.*

2 | *Put crocks or wire mesh over the drainage holes in the bottom to prevent the drainage holes from blocking up with soil.*

3 | *Add general purpose compost and plant with some colorful or edible plants.*

4 | *Water the plants in well, and then keep regularly watered during summer.*

MAINTENANCE

In a rooftop garden, vegetables should be regularly picked to keep them producing more, and ornamental plants will need deadheading for a continuation of the display. Keep plants well watered during summer. Due to their elevated situation, they can be more prone to drying out from the additional wind, so check regularly to ensure the soil hasn't dried out. As always, keep the beds free of weeds.

In large cities you can see impressive gardens built on huge roofs that are open to the public.

GREEN ROOFS

There has been a huge increase in the popularity of green roofs over the last couple of decades, driven by people's desire to beautify towns and urban spaces. Green roofs help to combat pollution and poor air quality. They are also a fantastic way of utilizing an otherwise unused and uninteresting space. Planting green roofs should help to attract wildlife and will also help to insulate your property if constructed on the house.

Where to create one

Most green roofs are created on flat roofs such as kitchen extensions on the back of the house. Garage roofs are also very popular. Shed roofs, with their sloping pitch providing natural drainage, are an excellent choice. Ideally the roof should be in full sun as this will give you a greater choice of plants to grow, although there is a huge range of shade-loving plants that can be selected, too.

How to create a green roof on a shed

1 | *Before you start, it is best to get advice from a structural engineer as to whether your building can support the weight on the roof.*

2 | *Measure the size of the roof and cut a sheet of marine plywood that fits the space.*

3 | *Cover the marine plywood with a butyl liner, or cheaper alternatives such as black sheeting, and attach it to the roof.*

4 | *Attach 3 inch cleats around the outside edges of the marine plywood to create a shallow planting frame.*

5 | *Fill the frame with a mix of general purpose soil, perlite, and rock wool (which makes the compost substrate much lighter, thereby reducing weight on the roof structure). For sempervivums, sedums, or salad leaf crops a depth of 3 inches should be sufficient; other crops may need deeper soil.*

6 | *Drill drainage holes in the bottom edge of the baton to prevent the bed becoming waterlogged. Plug them up with rock wool to prevent the growing medium washing out after rainfall.*

7 | *Plant the herbs or succulents into the growing medium at an equal spacing.*

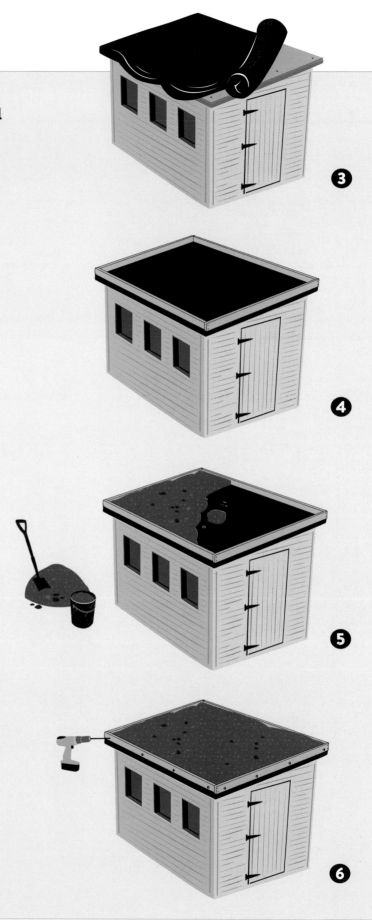

What to plant in a green roof

Low-growing plants that will hug the roof are ideal. The most commonly used plants are succulents such as sempervivums and sedums as they are fairly low maintenance—an important consideration if you are having to climb a ladder to reach them. However, you could consider planting perennial herbs such as thyme, marjoram, and prostrate forms of rosemary, which will tend to look after themselves. If you have easy access to the roof then you could try growing lettuce and salad crops, which will thrive in the shallow soil of a green roof. Avoid tall, upright vegetables that will get blown about in the wind.

Pre-planted

You can buy pre-planted mats that can simply be rolled out and attached to the roof. This is more expensive, but it does provide you with an instant display of colorful plants.

Vertical growing

If you don't have a space for a green roof, it is possible to grow crops up your walls and fences. There are fixtures and fittings that provide planting spaces to hang vertically. Some even come with irrigation systems so you don't have to worry about watering them. They are perfect for trailing plants such as tumbling tomatoes and strawberries.

MAINTENANCE

Traditionally, green roofs are planted with low-maintenance plants, which makes them easy to care for. However, weeds will attempt to colonize a green roof, so it will be necessary to access it two or three times over the summer to hand pull invading weeds, if you wish to keep your green roof weed free. Replace any plants that may have died after planting. If your bed is planted with succulents such as sedum and sempervivum then they shouldn't need watering often, but it is worth checking during periods of prolonged drought. Once a year, check the structure of the roof to ensure that the timber is still sound. If it is starting to rot, it should be replaced immediately.

TERRACED RAISED BEDS

Raised beds offer the perfect solution for gardening on steep slopes. Using the structure of the bed to level off the surface makes gardening much easier and also helps to retain moisture. On steep slopes water drains away quickly, often taking any nutrients and minerals with it. Seed will float down the hill, making it very difficult to grow plants from seed. Terraced raised beds can be made from any material, but lumber is easier than bricks as it can be cut more easily to adjust levels. However, the lumber needs to be thick and strong enough to support the weight of the soil on the lower side of the slope.

Raised beds offer the perfect solution for gardening on steep slopes.

MAINTENANCE

Due to the additional weight on the edging boards from the soil on a slope, they may need replacing more often than lumber in a raised bed on level ground, so do check them annually. Ensure the beds are kept weed free, so that your plants don't have to compete for nutrients. Mulch the beds, either with garden manure or other weed-suppressing material. As well as preventing weeds from germinating, this should help to retain moisture. Tall herbaceous plants will require staking to prevent them from flopping over, while plants such as sweet peas and roses will need deadheading to encourage them to continue flowering. Keep a vigilant watch for pests and diseases and try to spot symptoms early to prevent them destroying the plants. Soft fruit and vegetables will need to be covered with a net to prevent birds from eating the crops.

How to make a terraced raised bed

1 | *Begin by making a simple box-shaped frame out of the lumber, which will give you your front, back and sides. Screw them together.*

2 | *Place the wooden frame on the slope where it is to be built. Rest a level on the side of the frame, go down to the lower end, and lift the frame up so that the bubble in the level sits in the middle. The frame should now be level from top to bottom of the slope. Place blocks of wood or bricks under the frame to temporarily hold it in place.*

3 | *Next, place the level on the end of the frame at the lowest end, and adjust the height of the frame to the left and right until the bubble is in the middle of the level. Again, place blocks under the frame to temporarily hold it in place.*

4 | *Use wooden corner pegs and drive them into the inside corners. Use a rubber mallet to bang them into the ground. Screw them to the edging boards. You can then take away the temporary blocks and the frame should stand level on its own.*

5 | *Take a length of board the same length as the side and place it along the outside edge of one of the sides so that it is flush with the ground. On the inside of the frame use a pencil to mark down its entire length where it needs to be cut.*

6 | *Use a bandsaw, jigsaw, or chainsaw (remember to wear gloves) to cut down the length of the wood, following the pencil mark.*

7 | *Screw this length of wood to the corner posts. Repeat the process on the other side of the frame. There should now be no gaps on the sides of the level frame.*

8 | *To fill in the gap at the bottom of the lower slope, take a length of board the same length as the lower end section. Place it on the outside of the frame and then use a pencil to make a line on the inside. Use a saw to cut along the edge of the board and screw it to the end corner posts.*

9 | *To prevent the frame from bowing, drive in more wooden stakes alongside the inside of the frame at 3 foot intervals and screw them to the edges of the boards.*

10 | *Fill the raised bed with topsoil or compost to just below the top edge of the raised bed. You are now ready to start planting or sowing.*

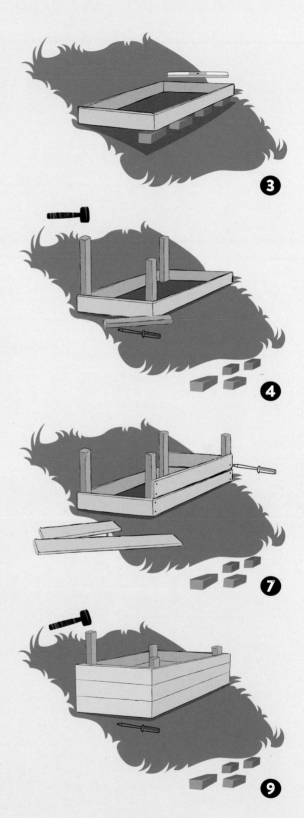

ALPINE RAISED TROUGH GARDEN

Alpine gardens are increasingly popular. Not only is there a great range of plants to choose from, but most of them require very little maintenance. Alpine plants are small, so they take up very little space. This makes them ideal for small gardens, courtyards, and in particular for growing in raised beds. Alpine plants usually require well-drained soil, which is another benefit of growing them in a raised bed, where the moisture drains away faster than if they were planted directly in the soil. And because the plants are very small, often clinging to the ground, it is easier to see them, and work with them, if they are that bit higher.

What is alpine?

Originally the term "alpine" was used to refer to plants originating from the mountainous Alps region of Europe. These days, it is used to describe any plants that hail from high elevations above the treeline.

MAINTENANCE

Looking after alpine plants couldn't be simpler. They shouldn't need watering as they are fairly drought-tolerant plants. Occasionally weeds may need to be pulled up. The succulents will need dividing, propagating, and replanting every few years.

How to make an alpine raised trough garden

Alpine plants can easily be grown in any of the raised beds described in this book, but specialist growers often like to grow them in sinks with lots of gritty soil. However, they can be hard to come by—this small concrete raised bed made with coir fiber makes a great alternative for growing alpines in, looking like an authentic stone trough.

1 | To make the concrete trough, create a mix of two parts coir fiber, one part cement, and one part sharp sand. Add water to make the mixture into a workable paste.

2 | Take a large cardboard box and fill the bottom 1.5 inches of it with the concrete mixture.

3 | Cut a wire mesh grid to fit the size of the bottom of the cardboard box and lay it on top of the mixture. Add another three quarters of an inch of the mixture to the bottom so that the mesh is covered. This mesh should give extra strength to the base of the trough.

4 | Push five or six wooden dowels through the base of the mixture—later these will become drainage holes.

5 | Place another cardboard box inside the existing box. This second box needs to be about 2 inches smaller on all sides. Place bricks on the bottom to act as weights.

6 | Cut more wire mesh grids and slide them down the side of the outer box, ensuring that it is shorter than the sides of the cardboard, so that it doesn't show.

7 | Pack the concrete mixture down the sides between the boxes, using a small stick to tamp it all down. Add more bricks to the inner box to add pressure to the sides of the box.

8 | Leave the container for a couple of days until the concrete has set. Then remove all of the cardboard and you should be left with a lovely looking concrete container.

9 | Knock out the dowels to form the drainage holes. The sides can be scored to look aged. Alternatively, coat it with natural yogurt to encourage algae and lichen to grow on it.

10 | Place the stone trough on four bricks, one at each corner, to assist with drainage.

11 | Fill the trough with a 50:50 mix of topsoil and horticultural grit.

12 | Plant alpine plants in the top, such as sempervivums, sedums and echeverias.

Part 3:
PLANTS AND PROJECTS

There is nothing more rewarding than creating your own raised beds and then packing them full of your favorite plants, whether they be fruit trees, vegetables, ornamentals, or even aquatic plants for a raised pond. In this chapter you'll find lots of ideas and inspiration to show you how to create a beautiful, vibrant display, whether you have a large garden, courtyard, balcony, or just a window box.

STRAWBERRIES ON PLANKS

This must be the simplest type of raised bed. It is literally just strawberries, grown in growing bags, or compost bags, and placed onto lengths of planks, supported by stacks of bricks or plastic crates.

Cost saving

If you look carefully, you will probably be able to find the material to construct these beds for free, meaning your only cost will be the cost of the soil and strawberry plants. Planks and old plastic or wooden crates can often be found in dumpsters or being thrown out around the back of factories or warehouses. Breeze blocks or recycled bricks can also be found easily. In fact, if you have a friend already growing strawberries, you can get free plants too by removing runners (the long shoots attached to the plants) and by planting them up, they will develop into strawberry plants.

Labor saving

Anybody who has grown strawberries before directly in the ground, while enjoying the delicious fruit, will also appreciate the back-breaking effort it can be. As they are such low growing plants, it means that any type of maintenance such as weeding or harvesting involves bending over, right down to ground level. Not a comfortable position to be in! Furthermore, strawberries on the ground are far more prone to slug and snail damage if grown directly in the soil. Using raised planks saves having to place straw under the plants to prevent them rotting on the ground, and their natural trailing habit means that they are ideal for hanging off the sides of the planks of wood.

MAINTENANCE

Plants in growing bags will need watering most days during the summer. They will also need a liquid feed every week once the fruits start to form.

Growing bags will need replacing each year. The plants can be saved and placed into fresh growing bags in early spring. Renew the plants every three years.

Fruits are ready for harvesting when they have turned red all over and are very slightly soft to the touch.

Which variety?

There are two different types of strawberries: summer fruiting ones and perpetuals (sometimes called everbearers). Perpetuals produce fruit from early summer through to mid autumn. The summer fruiting types produce larger fruits but only for a period of two or three weeks during the early part of summer. These types are divided up into early, mid, and late season. Selecting a few of each type will ensure a regular supply of fruit throughout the summer.

How to grow strawberries on planks

1 | *Start by constructing the raised plank beds. Stack crates or bricks about 6 feet apart, to a height of about 3 feet, or to whatever height feels comfortable to you.*

2 | *Place the planks on top of the stacks of crates or bricks, ensuring they are level.*

3 | *Take a growing bag, turn it on its side, and bang it to loosen the compost in the bag.*

4 | *Turn the growing bag onto its back on the plank and then, using a knife, make three equally spaced holes in the surface.*

5 | *Plant the strawberry plants into the holes in the growing bag, ensuring that the crown is just below the surface of the soil.*

6 | *Water the plants thoroughly. Repeat the process with more growing bags and place them end to end along the planks of wood.*

Planting project:

HERB GARDEN

*It's almost impossible to grow a bed of herbs without it looking fantastic.
They are also, fortunately, very easy to nurture provided you meet their basic needs:
most of them prefer a warm site that is in full sun.*

Grown in a raised bed, their requirements for good drainage are also met, and harvesting them will be an absolute joy — already at tabletop height, they are within easy reach. Some, such as mint, are a bit too vigorous for their own good, so a small raised bed devoted entirely to these rapidly spreading herbs is a good idea. Alternatively, for mint, you could use partitions to grow several different varieties in one single bed.

Herb gardens are very often grown in either a formal style, in a number of symmetrical beds lined with edging plants, or simply as an informal herb patch. The lines and edges of a raised bed lend themselves very well to a formal layout, so let these dictate the pattern of planting. A circular keyhole bed, for example, would lend itself perfectly to a cartwheel design.

Here is a suggestion for planting your own herb garden, based on a rectangular raised bed 4 feet by 6 feet with a central composting basket. Chives are used for edging, but alternative edging herbs include lavender, parsley, sage, or santolina. Only edge large raised beds with shrubby herbs like lavender, otherwise they will take up all the space.

PLANTING SUGGESTIONS:

- **For the edging:** Chives (*Allium schoenoprasum*) x 48
- **For bed 1:** Basil (*Ocimum basilicum*) x 1
  Marjoram (*Origanum vulgare*) x 3
- **For bed 2:** Hyssop (*Hyssopus officinalis*) x 1
  Wild thyme (*Thymus serpyllum*) x 2
  Silver variegated thyme (*Thymus vulgaris* 'Silver Posie') x 2
  Golden thyme (*Thymus* 'Doone Valley') x 2
- **For bed 3:** Variegated sage (*Salvia officinalis* 'Icterina') x 1
  Parsley (*Petroselinum crispum*) x 5
- **For bed 4:** Dill (*Anethum graveolens*) x 1
  Chervil (*Anthriscus cerefolium*) x 3
  Coriander (*Coriandrum sativum*) x 3

1 | Plant an edging of chives around the central composting basket, and then around the four edges of the raised bed. Then divide the growing area into four clearly defined sections with the remaining chives.

2 | In each of the four sections you will have enough space to grow two or three different types of herb. Arrange the taller single herb at the center of each quarter section, and the lower herbs around it.

3 | Water the herbs in well and when they are established clip, trim, or harvest their leaves regularly to keep them fresh and compact.

Coriander · Chives · Chervil · Basil · Dill · Marjoram · Parsley · Hyssop · Variegated sage · Golden thyme · Silver variegated thyme · Wild thyme

Maintenance

At the end of the growing season, tidy the herb bed by removing any dead growth. The annual herbs—coriander, chervil, and dill—will die back at this time of year so remove them completely, disposing of all material in the compost bin. The gaps created could be filled the following spring with different herbs to vary the display. Early next spring, clip back the shrubby herbs as close as you can so that they remain compact.

MAKING A FORMAL POND

Raised beds don't have to be filled with soil or compost. They can, of course, be filled with water and packed with attractive and colorful aquatic plants. Raised ponds are useful if you have small children as it is not so easy for them to fall in. They also raise the height of the aquatic life up closer to eye level. Raised ponds can have seating around the outside, which makes a lovely place to sit and gaze down into the water.

Siting your pond

There is nothing better than a water feature in the garden, whether it is for attracting frogs, newts, and other wildlife or for just lazy days staring at reflections and the light and shade playing on the surface of the water. If formal ponds are placed in direct sunlight they can be prone to a lot of algae, making the water green, so it is a good idea to place one in dappled light. Think about the positioning carefully. Do you want to access all sides of the pond? Do you want to make a central feature or focal point out of it, in which case, you will want to place it in the center of the garden and have paths leading up towards it? Alternatively, you may wish it to be something that you come across as you walk around the garden, in which case you may wish to think of screening or hedging to create a secluded corner somewhere.

How to make a formal pond

Formal ponds imply straight lines and a sense of symmetry to the design. They can be built out of bricks, rocks, or lumber. The project below is made out of railroad ties because it is so simple to build, and the chunky, wide lumber also provides a great place to sit. Avoid using recycled railway ties as they will leach out creosote and tar in warm weather, which could affect the wildlife in the pond. It will also make a mess of your clothes if you sit on it.

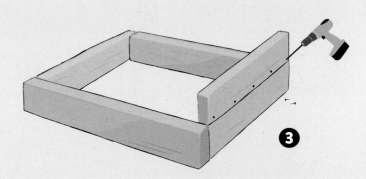

1 | Lay the ties on their edge out on the ground in the shape of a rectangle where you intend to have the raised pond. Make sure that the ground is level using a level tool.

2 | Screw through the corners of the ties to attach them to each other. Screws should go in at least 2 inches into the other board.

3 | If you intend to create more layers of ties then place them on top. Rather than using massive screws to drill through the top of one tie into the one below, it is easier to drill down at 45 degrees through the side of the top railroad tie and into the lower one.

4 | Once you have the right height for the raised pond, use an old carpet to lay across the floor and sides of the pond, to prevent sharp edges such as stones puncturing the pond liner.

5 | Place the liner in the bottom of the pond and up the sides. To hold the liner in place, attach another railroad tie to create a top layer and hide the pond liner. There are lots of different types of pond liners available from garden centers and specialist aquatic centers, or online. Liners vary in quality and thickness. At the cheaper end are PVC liners, but the best ones are rubber based, made from butyl.

6 | Fill the pond up with water to the height of the liner.

7 | Add oxygenating plants and other aquatic plants. You can also introduce fish such as koi carp to your pond, should you want to.

Aquatic plants for your pond

Oxygenating plants (also called submerged plants) are placed under the water. As their name suggests, they release oxygen, helping to keep the water clean and prevent it from turning green. Some oxygenators can become invasive if left to their own devices—you may need to occasionally lift them out, cut them back by half and replace the remainder in the water. Popular plants include:

- *Callitriche hermaphroditica* (water starwort)
- *Fontinalis antipyretica* (willow moss)
- *Hippuris vulgaris* (mare's tail)
- *Lobelia dortmanna* (water lobelia)
- *Ranunculus aquatilis* (water crowfoot)

Floating plants don't root in the soil but float on the surface or just below it, helping to reduce the pond's exposure to direct sunlight, which in turn helps to reduce the growth of algae. Aim for about 50 percent coverage of the surface of the water with plants. Popular plants include:

- *Azolla mexicana* (Mexican water fern)
- *Hydrocharis morsus-ranae* (frogbit)
- *Stratiotes aloides* (water soldier)

Water lilies are the quintessential pond plant with their attractive flower heads and broad leaves that float on the surface. They vary in the depth they need to be planted in the pond, so check with the aquatic nursery or plant center before purchasing to ensure it is suitable for your pond. Popular plants include:

- *Nymphaea alba* (white water lily)
- *N. 'Amabilis'*
- *N. 'Gladstoneana'*
- *N. 'Gonnère'*
- *N. 'James Brydon'*
- *N. 'Rose Arey'*
- *N. 'William Falconer'*
- *N. 'Aurora'*
- *N. odorata* var. *minor*
- *N. tetragona*

Marginal aquatics are usually planted in aquatic pots on the shelves at the edge of the pond, usually between 2-4 inches deep. The depth can be reduced on the marginal shelf by placing the plants on bricks. They provide a decorative quality to the pond, soften the edges, and provide a habitat for wildlife. Popular plants include:

- *Calla palustris* (bog arum)
- *Caltha palustris* (marsh marigold)
- *Iris pseudacorus* (yellow flag)
- *Lobelia cardinalis* (bog sage)
- *Lysichiton americanus* (yellow skunk cabbage)
- *Myosotis scorpiodies* (water forget-me-not)

MAINTENANCE

Keep an eye out for invasive weeds such as duckweed and blanket weed and use a net to remove it as soon as you spot it.

If the water is turning green then a bundle of barley straw can be placed in the pond which should help re-oxygenate the water.

In hot weather the pond may need topping off with water as it evaporates under the sun. If possible, have a rain barrel nearby for such eventualities.

Plants will occasionally need lifting out of the pond, dividing and repotting before placing them back in the water.

POND LIFE

Fish are a wonderful addition to any garden pond. Not only do they add movement and color, they also help to keep mosquito and gnat larvae populations under control. However, do be careful not to overstock the pond. As a rule of thumb there should be no more than 1 inch of fish per 13 gallons of water. It is better to under stock, to allow for fish to grow and develop to a decent size. Always ensure there is plenty of plant cover and oxygenating plants in the pond for the fish.

Planting project:

FRONT GARDEN RAISED BED

· ·

Many front gardens in overcrowded urban areas are converted to driveways due to a shortage of street parking. A raised bed can turn this practical space into an attractive and welcoming feature.

A well-tended front-of-house raised bed improves your property's "curb appeal," increasing its desirability and therefore its value. It also provides a habitat for wildlife, encouraging butterflies, bees, and many other creatures to pay a visit.

When choosing material for the front garden raised bed, select wood or bricks that are in keeping with the house, otherwise they will look out of place. The choice of plants is equally important: they need to be tough and pollution tolerant if your house is on a busy road. If you are short of space, then the beds need to be as narrow as possible to allow space for a car. Having a raised bed means that you will also be able to see the plants from your front windows, possibly even while sitting on your sofa.

PLANTING SUGGESTIONS:

- *Hypericum* 'Hidcote' (St. John's wort)
- *Buddleja davidii* 'Royal Red' (butterfly bush)
- *Philadelphus* 'Beauclerk' (mock orange)
- *Ribes sanguineum* (flowering currant)
- *Sambucus nigra* 'Black Lace' (elderberry)
- *Amelanchier lamarckii* (juneberry)
- *Euonymus fortunei* 'Emerald Green' (spindle)
- *Aucuba japonica* (Japanese laurel)

1 | Measure up your space and ensure you leave plenty of room to park your car and get out of the doors either side. Bear in mind that visitors to your house may have wider cars than you. The bed(s) will need to be made to fit the individual space. Two beds are ideal, one on either side of your parking space.

2 | Create a mix of 50:50 organic matter and topsoil and fill up the beds.

3 | Place a black landscape fabric over the soil and pin it down with pegs. This will help to suppress weeds.

4 | Choose drought-tolerant shrubs and plant them 3 feet apart. Use a knife to cut through the fabric to create the planting hole.

5 | Cover the black landscape fabric with mulch to give it a natural look.

The circular chart is labelled with the following plant names around its perimeter:

- St John's wort
- Buddleja
- Japanese laurel
- Mock orange
- Spindle
- Flowering currant
- Juneberry
- Elderberry

Maintenance

These are low-maintenance beds and the black landscape fabric should help to suppress any weeds. The mulch will occasionally need topping off, though. Keep the plants regularly watered during their first year of planting from spring through to midsummer.

WILDLIFE POND

There is nothing quite as beautiful as a wildlife pond in the garden, and this is enhanced when creating one within a raised bed as it brings it closer to eye level. It will attract bees, butterflies, dragonflies, and lots of other fascinating insects, as well as creating an informal feature that will be packed full of wildflowers creating a cacophony of color and texture.

Raise it up

Wildlife ponds can, of course, be created at ground level, which is beneficial for small mammals that can approach the sides of the ponds. However, by raising the pond up higher, it creates a safer environment for birds and, of course, it makes it easier to manage and maintain. Also, if you only have a small garden or courtyard with a concrete or hard surface, you will have no option but to build it off the ground.

The natural look

The trick with creating a wildlife pond is to not make it look too contrived. Planting should look natural and the shape of the pond should be informal, as if nature itself had shaped it, rather than a gardener with a spade. Avoid symmetry. Bricks and lumber can be used to create the raised bed but for a really informal section a woven willow fence looks in keeping and, because of its flexibility, you can use it to create curves and naturalistic, informal shapes. You could also try using a living willow weave, cutting it back each year. The willow shoots will add to the natural, watery feel.

MAINTENANCE

Thankfully, wildlife gardens tend to look after themselves and you shouldn't need to do much to maintain it. It shouldn't look over manicured. However, do look out for invasive weeds that could take over, and remove them as soon as they are spotted.

Create some ramps for hedgehogs and other small mammals to climb up to drink from the pond. Ramps should also lead into the pond from the surface of the raised bed. Disguise the ramps with plants to protect them from predators.

When the flowers and grass around the outside of the pond start to die back, they can be cut down to tidy the beds up. The material should be removed and added to the compost heap. However, do leave some seed heads and other material for the wildlife. Some will need it for overwintering.

Place bird boxes on nearby trees or fences as birds will be attracted to the pond and start using it.

How to create a wildlife pond

1 | *Mark out where you want the raised bed to be using sand or a hose, taking care to create a natural, curvy, informal shape.*

2 | *Bang in sturdy wooden posts along the shape of the pond at 30 inch intervals. The posts need to be firm as they will need to support the weight of the soil of the raised wildlife pond.*

3 | *Weave the willow branches between the stakes as shown on page 83.*

4 | *Don't make the raised bed any higher than about 2 feet as the woven structure won't be strong enough to support the soil. Fill the structure in with soil and firm it down.*

5 | *Mark out within the soil where the pond will be created. Dig out the shape to about 18 inches in the center, leaving a shelf around the outside that is about 8 inches wide and 8 inches below the surface of the pond for marginal plants. Leave plenty of room in the bed around the outside of the pond for planting other plants.*

6 | *Spread carpet or a ¾ inch layer of soft sand into the bottom of the hole to avoid any stones or sharp objects puncturing the liner.*

7 | *Place a butyl pond liner into the bottom and up the sides. Hold down the sides of the liner by placing soil on top of the liner, which will also help hide it.*

8 | *Fill up the pond with water to the height of the liner.*

9 | *Place marginal plants on the shelf of the pond and deeper aquatic plants in the center.*

10 | *Rake over soil around the outskirts of the pond and sow either grass seed or a wildflower mix into it.*

11 | *If space allows, you could also plant a small tree or a shrub by the side of the pond in the raised bed to create some shade over the pond and to make additional habitat for wildlife.*

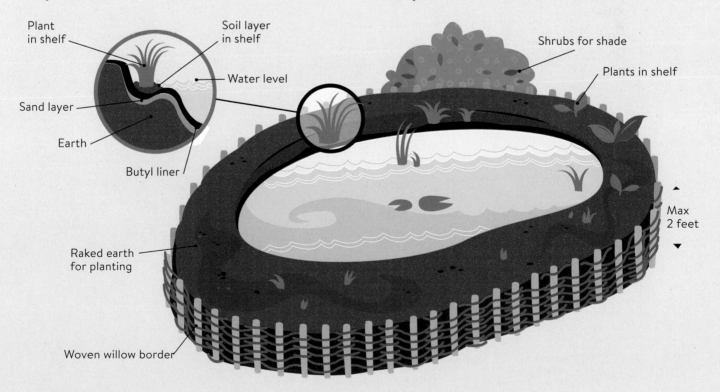

Plant in shelf

Soil layer in shelf

Water level

Sand layer

Earth

Butyl liner

Shrubs for shade

Plants in shelf

Max 2 feet

Raked earth for planting

Woven willow border

Planting project:
RAISED DAHLIA BED

If you want to create an impressive bright splash of color in your garden, dahlias are the ideal flowering plant for you. These herbaceous perennials produce a range of show-stopping, flamboyant flowers in almost every color imaginable.

Originating from Mexico, dahlias prefer to be planted in full sunshine, but will tolerate a moderate amount of shade. However, they hate being in wet soil as their tuberous root systems will start to rot, so good drainage is the key to successfully growing them. Raised beds provide an ideal solution for gardens with heavy, clay soil, as the elevation helps to allow excess moisture to flow away, and enables you to add compost or soil with better drainage qualities. Dahlias are susceptible to slugs and snails, so damage should be limited by growing them off the ground. Rabbits have a tendency to dig up the edible tubers—putting them out of their reach should help to prevent this from happening.

PLANTING SUGGESTIONS:

There are so many different varieties of dahlia, the hard part will be choosing which ones to include in your bed.

1 | Build your raised bed. Any shape of bed will do, but ensure it is raised off the ground by at least a foot if the garden has poor soil, to increase drainage.

2 | Fill the raised bed with a good quality compost or topsoil and add horticultural grit to create a 50:50 mix. This should improve the drainage and prevent the tuberous root rotting.

3 | Choose a range of different varieties. There are lots to choose from, but get a mix to maximize the effect. Don't worry about clashing colors; with dahlias it adds to the bright, cheerful effect.

4 | Plant dahlia tubers out when the risk of frost is over, at a distance of about 20 inches between each tuber, depending on the variety. They should be at a depth of 4-6 inches below the soil surface.

5 | Water the tubers in well, and keep them well watered until they start to send out new growth. From then on only water them every few days if the weather remains dry.

Maintenance

As the tubers start to grow their tips should be pinched out to encourage a bushier plant that will produce more flowers. This is usually when they reach a height of about 15 inches. Use a pair of pruners and cut back to a healthy pair of leaves.

For maximum effect, only retain five or six shoots growing directly off the main stem. This will ensure the flowers get to a good size and don't become too overcrowded. Remove any excess shoots at the base.

As the dahlias start to grow, they will need staking to prevent the large flower heads from flopping over.

Feed dahlias once every two weeks during summer with a balanced liquid fertilizer.

If you live in USDA hardiness zones 7 or lower, then the tubers should be dug up from the soil once the foliage starts to blacken in autumn. Take them into a shed and hang them upside down to dry for a week or two, allowing any excess moisture to drain away. Then place them into boxes and cover with sand or compost for the winter and keep them in a frost-free place such as a garden shed or greenhouse. Plant them outside again in late spring once the risk of frost is over.

If you garden in USDA zones 8 or higher, it isn't necessary to dig up the dahlias; simply cut back the foliage once it has blackened. Covering the soil above the tuber with an additional 3 inches of mulch will help to provide extra protection.

MAKING A BUBBLE FOUNTAIN

For those people without room for a full-sized pond, it is still possible to incorporate a water feature in the garden by installing a bubble fountain. Placing it in the middle of a raised bed makes it easier to see, and creates an interesting focal point. It offers the relaxing tinkling sound of water and adds movement and vibrancy to an outdoor space. There is nothing more peaceful and relaxing than the sound of running water on a hot summer's day, and the movement also captures the sunlight creating an enchanting vibrancy to the garden.

MAINTENANCE

There is very little maintenance required for this raised bubble feature. The pump will occasionally need its filter washed out, removing any dirt or other debris. Keep an eye on the level of water in the container, particularly in hot weather, as it will quickly evaporate. If there isn't enough water to cover the water pump, it will be damaged when switched on.

Frisbee water feature

For the ultimate mini water feature, place a Frisbee rim-side up on your window ledge. (If you don't have a Frisbee, a plate or bowl will work just as well.) Add some pebbles and top off with water. The pebbles will enable bees and other insects to land and drink without drowning. Alternatively, fill it with soil and sprinkle cress seeds on top of it for the ultimate mini raised bed.

How to create a bubble fountain

You could, of course, purchase a ready-made bubble fountain, but it is just as easy to create your own raised mini water feature. You will need a submersible pump, connected to a safe electricity source. Submersible pumps are available online or from garden centers and water garden specialists. They vary in power and the volume, or flow, of water they can pump, so ensure you purchase one that will be enough to circulate the water. For this project you will need a pump with a telescopic fountain so that the water can be pumped upwards to create the bubble effect. A large plant container is used in the project below, but you could easily use old wooden barrels or other large containers if you have more space.

1 | Choose a container that suits the style of your house or garden. It should be tall and wide enough to incorporate the submersible pump.

2 | Use the drainage hole to feed the electric cable through for the pump and keep it hidden. The container will need to be raised on feet or bricks so that the weight of it doesn't sit on the cable.

3 | Once the cable has been fed through, the hole should be sealed to make it watertight.

4 | The pump should be placed in the center of the bottom of the container. The telescopic attachment must be level with the top of the stones, which will be added in step 7. If the pump is too low, it can be placed on a small plant pot to raise it up.

5 | The pump should come with some fountain telescopic attachments, which can be fitted at this stage.

6 | Place a wire grill above the pump about halfway down in the container.

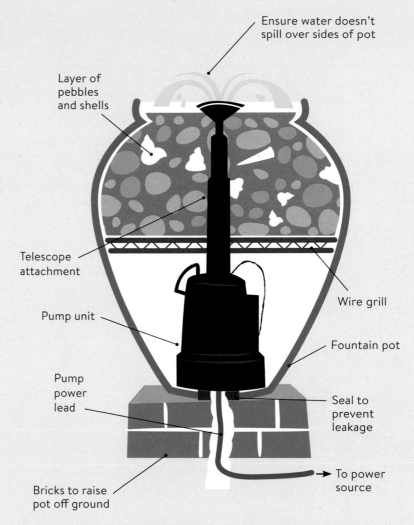

Ensure water doesn't spill over sides of pot

Layer of pebbles and shells

Telescope attachment

Pump unit

Pump power lead

Bricks to raise pot off ground

Wire grill

Fountain pot

Seal to prevent leakage

To power source

7 | Now fill the container up to the top with pebbles or shells, ensuring that the fountain head protrudes through the top.

8 | Fill the container with water, turn on the pump, and check that you are happy with the height of the water fountain. Make sure that it doesn't spurt out so high that the water is spilled outside of the container, as this will result in a rapid loss of water.

Planting project:
SINGLE-COLOR THEME

Designing a raised bed using plants of a single color is a useful technique for introducing harmony and simplicity into the garden. It avoids clashing contrasts and instead relies on variations of texture. Probably the most famous mono-colored garden is the White Garden designed by Vita Sackville-West at Sissinghurst, in Kent, England. Although we don't all have a garden as grand as this, similar principles can be used to create an impressive raised bed using just one color.

There are lots of white flowering plants available, so this is just a suggestion below, but any of them can be swapped for similar white flowering plants. This is for a bed measuring 10 feet by 10 feet, so the number of plants required can be varied for different sized borders.

Any of the different types of raised bed featured in this book would be suitable for this type of border. To maximize the effect of the plants at the right height, it should be built to about 20 inches.

PLANTING SUGGESTIONS:

- *Dianthus* 'Mrs Sinkins' (pinks) x 5
- *Erigeron karvinskianus* (Mexican fleabane) x 10
- *Astilbe* 'Deutschland' (astilbe) x 3
- *Hydrangea paniculata* 'White Moth' (hydrangea) x 1
- *Geranium sanguineum* 'Album' (bloody cranesbill) x 3
- White *Astrantia* (masterwort) x 3
- *Wisteria frutescens* 'Nivea' (wisteria) x 1
- *Dahlia* 'Bishop of Dover' (dahlia) x 3
- *Leucanthemum* 'Wirral Supreme' (shasta daisy) x 3

1 | Fill up the bed with soil to just below the top of the raised bed.
2 | Dig in plenty of organic matter such as garden compost or rotted manure.
3 | Plant the erigeron, dianthus, and geranium around the edge of the border.
4 | Behind it plant the dahlia, leucanthemum, and astilbe.
5 | Finally plant the hydrangea shrub in the center of the bed for mid to late summer interest. An alternative would be the white flowering shrub philadelphus (mock orange) for spring interest.

As an additional feature, if you have room, you can erect an archway and train a wisteria or summer jasmine up it. Alternatively, if you have a wall at the back, they can be trained up on a system of trellises or wires.

The circular wheel is labeled clockwise from top: Dahlia, Pinks, Mexican fleabane, Geranium, Hydrangea, Shasta daisy, Masterwort, Wisteria, Astilbe

Maintenance

The herbaceous plants can be cut down to near ground level once they have finished flowering in autumn.

The dahlia tubers should be dug up and stored over winter in a cool, frost-free, dark place in a box of sand or compost if living in an area prone to frosts.

To get really impressive, large flower spikes on your hydrangea shrubs the previous year's growth should be cut back to two buds.

Some of the taller herbaceous plants may need staking to prevent them from flopping over.

MAKING A SEATING AREA AROUND A RAISED BED

Part of the pleasure of creating a garden of raised beds is finding somewhere to sit and enjoy it. Being seated in among the plants brings you even closer to the plants, literally placing them right under your nose, rewarding you with an intoxicating, sensory overload.

Planning perfection

Creating a seating area requires careful planning to get it right. If you garden in a community garden then you need to consider whether you want a quiet secluded spot away from prying eyes and neighboring gardeners. However, many people have a community garden plot for the social aspect of sharing and exchanging gardening tips, in which case you might want to place your seat where you can chat to people passing by. In backyards you will probably want privacy from the neighbors. You may already have a secluded spot, or you might need to create one either with screening with plants, or with an overhead arbor.

Creating a rustic arbor

To create privacy and shade for the seat, a small arbor can be erected around it. These are easy to make and can be used to plant climbers up. Do be aware, though, that it could create shade over the raised beds, so if possible place the seat and arbor on the north side of the bed.

1 | Measure out where your four wooden upright posts are going to go to create the corners of the arbor around the bench.

2 | Use a spade to dig out the holes. The posts should be at least 16 inches into the ground.

3 | Place the posts in the hole and backfill around them with the soil, firming the soil in with your feet as you go. Regularly check that the posts are still at the same height and that they are upright with a level.

4 | Attach crossbars to link up the tops of the posts using long nails or screws.

5 | Attach trellis systems to the side of the arbor.

6 | Plant climbers such as honeysuckle or clematis around the sides of the arches. These will scramble up the structure, providing a wonderful leafy place to sit, and they will fill the air with fragrance with their flowers.

How to create a simple rustic bench

This is a very easy-to-make bench for perching on and resting your weary limbs after time spent gardening. Position it next to your raised bed to maximize the enjoyment of the garden. You will need two large, chunky logs and a wooden plank.

1 | Cut two large, chunky logs to the same height. These will be the two supports to the wooden seat so ensure that they are at a height that you are comfortable with. Bear in mind that the logs will be sunk about 12 inches into the ground.

2 | Work out the distance apart the two log supports are going to be, by laying the wooden plank or seat across it. Allow for an overhang of about 6 inches on either side.

3 | Dig out the holes for the logs, digging down to a depth of 12 inches.

4 | Place the logs in the holes and ensure that they are level with each other, otherwise you will have a wonky seat. Backfill around the holes using the soil from the hole and firm down the soil.

5 | Place the wooden plank onto the logs, check it is level again, and then screw the seat downwards into the logs using large, chunky screws. Use a wrench so that the head of the screw is countersunk just below the top of the bench.

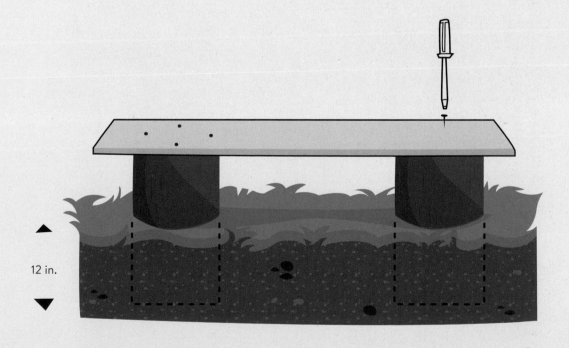

12 in.

Planting project:

JAPANESE GARDEN

There are so many fantastic plants that originate from Japan that you are spoilt for choice.

A traditional Japanese garden comprises certain key elements. A sense of peace and tranquillity is created in quiet corners set aside for contemplation. There is usually a water feature, either a pond filled with koi carp and arched red wooden bridges over it, or in smaller gardens a simple bubble fountain. Beds and paths are often mulched with gravel, with patterns raked into them.

This design incorporates most of the traditional elements but on a much smaller scale, to fit into a raised bed. Traditional Japanese plants such as azaleas and camellias require slightly acidic soil—compost to lower the pH can be easily incorporated into the soil in a raised bed.

PLANTING SUGGESTIONS:

- Clumping bamboo
- *Acer palmatum* (Japanese maple)
- Ornamental cherries
- Topiary
- Camellias and azaleas for structure
- Japanese ornamental grasses
- Closer to the ground, hostas and Japanese anemones are typical, but there are loads more than can be used including ferns, grasses, and mosses.

1 | Create a simple timber bed from gravel boards (see page 89). To give it a more Japanese feel, rolls of bamboo (available in most garden centers and hardware stores) can be nailed to the outside of the boards, or to be really authentic, bamboo canes can be woven through supporting upright, sturdy bamboo stakes, in a similar way to the willow raised bed (see page 83).

2 | If there is a wall or fence at the back of the raised bed, use bamboo panels to disguise it.

3 | Toward the back of the raised bed, plant a Japanese maple, *Acer palmatum*. This tree will grow to about 15 feet eventually, so in smaller spaces choose *Acer palmatum* 'Dissectum Atropurpureum',

which should only grow to half the height.

4 | Select some bamboos to place to the sides of the tree. Choose clump-forming types to avoid them spreading and taking over the garden. So for a nice contrast try *Phyllostachys nigra*, with its black, polished canes, and the yellow canes of *Phyllostachys aureosulcata* f. *spectabilis*. These add evergreen structural interest to the garden.

5 | At the base of the Japanese maple plant hostas, which should thrive in the shade of the tree.

6 | Around the front or edges of the raised bed plant two or three low-growing deciduous azaleas.

7 | Plant a cluster of five Japanese blood red grasses (*Imperata cylindrica* 'Rubra') in a corner of the raised bed. These ornamental grasses with their bright red foliage will add an impressive splash of color to the design.

8 | If there is room, create a container bubble fountain (see page 125) to add movement and sound to the design.

9 | Finally, mulch any bare soil in the raised bed with white gravel.

Hostas

Cogon grass

Azaleas

Bamboo

Japanese maple

Maintenance

It is very easy to maintain this garden. Keep a check on the bamboo clump to ensure it doesn't overgrow its space.

Cut the hostas back each year when the foliage starts to die. When the new foliage appears in spring, keep a lookout for slugs and snails—they love to feed on this plant. Use beer traps or slug pellets to protect the plant.

Top off the gravel once a year to keep it looking fresh.

RAISED BED DINING AREA

Raised beds lend themselves very well to the production of food, so to use them to enclose an outdoor dining area seems obvious. The design can incorporate a cooking area, such as a barbecue, clay oven, or firepit, with the plants in the raised beds grown to provide the ingredients. Some ornamental plants included in the plantings will provide a congenial ambience. All green waste should be added to the compost heap.

Materials

The choice of construction materials for a raised bed dining area are very important, and must go beyond the purely functional. Aesthetics are key, and whether you choose a modern design with metal-edged beds, classic stone, or rustic wood is up to you. Functionality, however, must not be overlooked: have you allowed enough room for people to sit and move around? Are there enough surfaces for drinks and condiments? All of this can take up a considerable amount of room, so before you start make sure you allocate ample space.

Plants

In the raised beds themselves you will want to plant a happy mixture of vegetables and herbs so that you have just enough for the kitchen and just enough for show. It is a balance of productivity and ornament, and to achieve this include a few flowering plants, preferably edible ones, amongst the crops. If, through harvesting, you create patches of bare soil in your raised bed, be quick to replant; garden centers are a ready source of filler plants in the summer. Plants can also be used to create screening and shelter. If you are overlooked, or wish to provide shade, build some wire supports into your design so that not only can climbing plants be grown onto them, but also some kind of shade or awning can be attached.

Location

Perhaps the most important factor is to choose a site that is sheltered and intimate. Unless you plan to have a fully functioning kitchen built into the design, it pays for the dining area to be near the house so that you do not have to walk great distances every time you need something from the refrigerator, for example.

SOME EDIBLE ORNAMENTALS

1 | *Foeniculum vulgare* (fennel) ☐ 2 | *Beta vulgaris* 'Bright Lights' (Swiss chard)
3 | *Lactuca sativa* 'Freckles' (Freckles lettuce) ☐ 4 | *Capsicum annuum* (chilli peppers)
5 | *Ocimum basilicum* (purple basil) ☐ 6 | *Viola odorata* (pansy) ☐ 7 | *Tropaeolum majus* (nasturtium)
8 | *Hemerocallis* spp. (daylilies) ☐ 9 | *Tagetes patula* (French marigold)

Planting project:

ROSES

• •

Roses are quite fussy about the soil they grow in, requiring a heavy, rich soil and fertile ground. Raised beds provide the perfect solution for those people with impoverished soil in their garden. Another benefit is that by growing the roses higher off the ground, it is easier to appreciate their color and scent.

Roses come in all shapes and sizes, from huge rambling and climbing types to low-growing shrubby ones. They come in almost every range of color, except blue, and most of them provide an exquisite floral scent that perfumes the garden. There are thousands of roses to choose from, and new ones are produced each year from plant nurseries. It is generally thought that some of the older shrub roses have the best scent, but this isn't always the case. Visit public parks and gardens with rose gardens and write down the names of the ones that catch your eye. Some roses are prone to diseases such as blackspot and mildew, so it could be worth choosing varieties which have some resistance.

This rose garden is designed for a raised bed measuring 10 feet by 10 feet, but more or fewer plants can be added if you have different size beds. The style of raised bed is up to you, depending on what fits in with your existing garden.

PLANTING SUGGESTIONS:

- ▫ **Rambling/climbing rose:** 'Rambling Rector' or 'Graham Thomas' x 1
- ▫ **Shrub rose:** *Rosa mundi* or *Rosa rugosa* x 3
- ▫ **Hybrid tea rose:** 'Peace' or 'Double Delight' x 8. However, there are thosands of hybrid teas to choose from, so select a color and type that you like and that complements the existing plants in the remainder of the garden.

1 | In the center of the raised bed put in two vertical posts that are 6 feet apart and 6 feet tall.
2 | Attach an attractive black or white rope between the posts which sags slightly. This is referred to in gardening as a "swag."
3 | Plant a climbing or rambling rose at the base of one of the posts and tie it to the post with string.
4 | Plant four shrub roses around the climbing roses leaving a space of about 3 feet between plants.
5 | Around the sides of the beds plant hybrid tea roses, two on each side.

'Graham Thomas'

'Double Delight'

Rosa mundi

Maintenance

Roses will need to be pruned each year in winter to ensure they flower each summer. Dead, diseased, and dying wood should be removed, as should crossing branches. Hybrid teas are usually cut back quite hard, whereas shrub roses require a lighter prune. On climbers and ramblers, after three or four years remove some of the older wood and tie in new shoots.

Mulch the raised beds each year with more organic matter.

Roses may need feeding with a rose fertilizer in the growing season if their leaves look pale, or they're not putting on growth.

Deadhead the roses regularly throughout the growing season to ensure they produce more flowers. Use hand pruners and cut back to a fresh leaf about 3 inches behind the dead flower head.

SUNKEN BEDS

In a sunken bed, it is the gardener who is "raised" above the bed, allowing you to admire your plants from above. If the sunken garden is large enough for you to stand or sit in, everything else is raised up around you, giving you a whole new perspective on your garden. It can also add a sense of seclusion if your garden is overlooked by neighbors. Planting patterns, whether it be with foliage plants or flowers, stand out more when admired from above. As with raised beds, if the soil is poor in your garden, you have the opportunity to excavate and replace it with something more suitable for your chosen plants to grow in.

Why sunken beds?

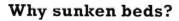

Sunken beds can be visually effective and are a useful technique for growing plants without impeding a view. They also offer a more fluid and dynamic feel to an outdoor space. In terms of design, it is exciting to notice plants that are only revealed to you once you come across them from above. They can also be beneficial if soil conditions are very dry. Planting deeper into the soil means the roots are closer to the water table. It can also act as a catchment to collect surface water, and because the wall of the sunken bed can shade some of the plants at the sides, it can reduce the need for watering. Planting in a sunken area is a practical solution to exposed sites where plants benefit from the added protection and shelter of being surrounded by walls.

How to create a simple sunken bed

Blueberries and cranberries like slightly damp and acidic soil. For people without these conditions in the garden, a sunken bed is an effective solution, meaning that these fresh superfruits can be harvested directly from their back or front garden. When purchasing plants, select varieties that will grow well in your area. There are blueberry types that are well suited for cooler climates and those that grow better in warmer areas.

1 | *Construct a wooden frame to fit the intended size and shape of your sunken garden.*

2 | *Place the wooden frame over the soil where the bed is to be constructed to act as a template. Excavate the soil and save it to use elsewhere in the garden. The depth should be just slightly less than the height of the wooden frame.*

3 | *Place the frame into the hole so that just sits just above the soil line by about ¾ inch. Drive in wooden stakes into each inside corner of the frame to hold it in position.*

4 | *Backfill using some of the spoil of the soil around the outside of the frame to help keep it secure.*

5 | *Lay a permeable landscape fabric across the bottom of the excavated bed and attach it to the inside of the frame using a staple gun.*

6 | *Pour compost into the bed, enough to fill it to your desired depth, and rake it level.*

7 | *Plant blueberries into the bed at a spacing of 4 feet between each plant. Cranberries are lower plants and can be planted around the outside of the bed at a spacing of 16 inches apart.*

MAINTENANCE

Plants will require watering in dry weather as they prefer slightly moist soil. Keep a rain barrel nearby as they should be watered with rainwater instead of tap water to avoid increasing the pH.

Cranberries require little maintenance, but they may occasionally need their straggly shoots tidied up with pruners or shears.

Blueberries should be pruned in wintertime. Remove some of the older wood at the base with loppers and try to retain young, new shoots.

Birds love blueberries, so cover the sunken bed with a net as soon as fruit starts to appear.

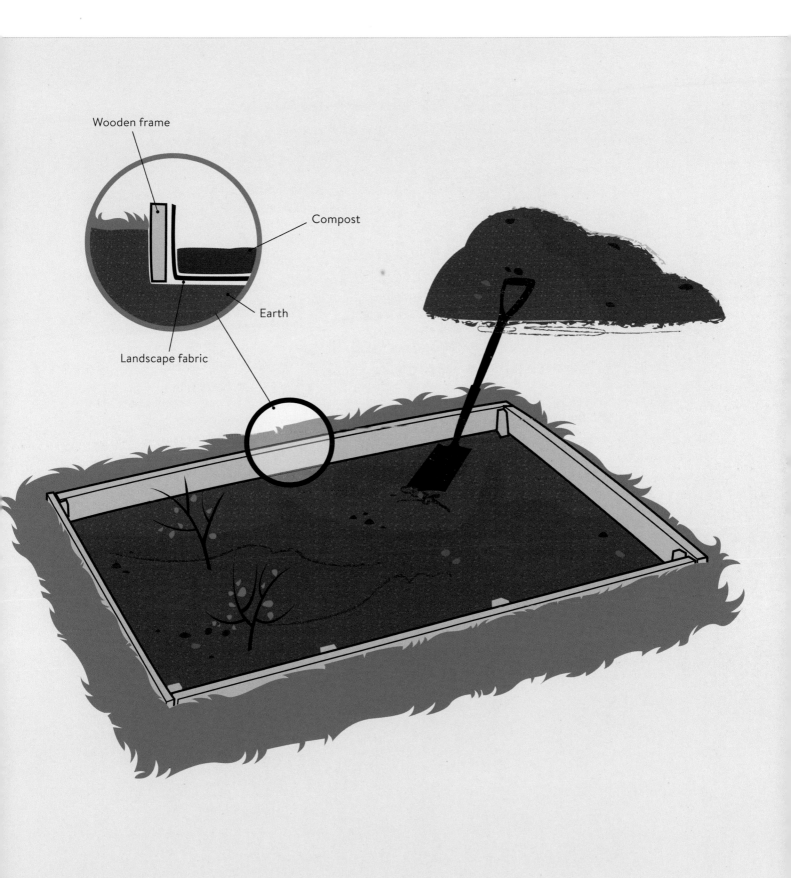

Wooden frame

Compost

Earth

Landscape fabric

Planting project:

PERMACULTURE RAISED BED

* *

Permaculture, or woodland kitchen gardening, is now increasing in popularity and a mini self-sufficient woodland can be created easily in a moderately sized raised bed.

What is permaculture?

The principles of permaculture rely on using three different tiers or different heights of canopies and plants, which are ground cover, shrubs, and small trees. All three levels provide a variety of habitats for wildlife and help to create a self-sustaining garden, whereby they all benefit from each other. The lower tier helps to suppress weeds while the highest tier provides dappled shade and prevents the woodland floor from drying out. The middle tier provides a link for small mammals and other wildlife between the top and bottom of the garden.

Because permaculture is based on natural woodland planting it looks great when planted in a very simplistic, rustic raised bed using lengths of logs or trunks for edging. It's a very rudimentary form of creating a raised bed, but it can look effective when planted up with fruiting shrubs and trees. It is best to use hardwood to create the raised beds, such as oak, beech, or ash as they will last for between five and ten years. Softwood will only last for about three.

PLANTING SUGGESTIONS:

- **Top level:** Apple trees, cherry trees, pear trees, plum trees, or hazel trees
- **Middle level:** Shrubs such as blueberries (if acidic enough soil), redcurrants, gooseberries, chokeberries, blackberries
- **Lower level:** Alpine strawberries, arctic raspberries, cranberries (if acidic soil)

1 | Place the logs in position and use stakes to hold them in place if necessary.
2 | Fill the bed up with soil to just below the top of the trunk.
3 | Space out the plants on the bed to ensure that they look right in the design. For example, you don't want the larger trees in the foreground and the ground cover at the back. Try to space them out so that the woodland feels balanced.
4 | Plant them in the soil and water them well.
5 | Cover the soil with woodchip mulch to suppress weeds and retain moisture.

Gooseberries

Alpine strawberries

Apples

Maintenance

This mini permaculture garden will require little maintenance, but it will need regular weeding to prevent them from taking over.

Some of the trees may need staking when they're young, particularly if they're on an exposed windy site.

Some of the shrubs and ground cover plants may need to be covered with a net if you want to harvest the fruit before the birds get to them.

FERNERY AND STUMPERY RAISED BED

Incredibly fashionable in Victorian times, ferneries and stumperies are now enjoying something of a revival in both the grounds of large stately homes and in small suburban back gardens and courtyards. Victorian plant hunters would bring back exciting new species of ferns. There is something intriguingly prehistoric about ferns; in fact, they were one of the first forms of plant life on the planet and as such it always feels special when you see them growing in the garden.

Why create a fernery and stumpery?

They offer all-year-round interest, with some ferns being evergreen while others provide exciting colors of greens, yellows, and coppers before dying back in late autumn. Stumps provide the backbone to a fernery, creating sculptural shapes which give a woodland feel to the design of the bed. They also provide the natural habitat for ferns, which are often found in dark, shady woodlands surrounded by decaying timber. Finally, these features are perfect for those dark, shady, damp areas of the garden that you don't know what to do with. Lots of ferns are low growing, so by planting them in a raised bed it elevates them so that they can be seen better. There is something magical about walking alongside raised beds filled with these woodland plants.

Sourcing stumps

If you live in a town then contact your local tree services as they will often be digging out stumps and will probably be more than happy to offload them. To expose a stump fully and see it in its full glory, it should be washed down with a pressure washer. If you wish to age it, you can use a paintbrush and coat it with live natural yogurt to encourage mosses and lichen to develop on it.

How to create a fernery and stumpery

1 | *Create a rustic raised bed using tree trunks laid on their side to form a square or rectangle.*

2 | *Fill the bed with soil but add leaf mold into the top spade depth of soil, to replicate the woodland conditions that ferns grow in.*

3 | *Place the stumps prior to planting. Give careful consideration to where they are placed, thinking of it like a painting composition, ensuring that the bed feels balanced with the right ratio of plants to stumps. There is no equation to work this out, it just needs to feel right.*

4 | *Plant the ferns into the soil (see below for a list of ferns to try), ideally keeping lower ones to the front and taller ones to the back, although it is good to vary this slightly. If the raised bed is designed to be walked all around, then taller ones should be in the middle.*

5 | *If you want to add splashes of color then you can also plant some bulbs such as narcissus or snowdrops, although do remember that the latter should always be planted in the green, i.e. when they're in leaf. Winter aconites also make an attractive feature to the woodland floor with their yellow bowl-shaped flowers.*

Ferns to try

Adiantum pedatum (maidenhair fern) is an attractive deciduous maidenhair fern which will quickly form clumps reaching about 8 inches tall.

Dicksonia antarctica (tree fern) is ideal for adding height to the back of the border. They can reach as high as 10 feet.

Dryopteris erythrosora (Japanese sheild fern) is an evergreen shrub with tall, elegant fronds that are orange when they emerge and become bright green as they mature, reaching about 2 feet in height.

Polystichum setiferum (soft shield fern) retains its fronds throughout winter until the new ones emerge in spring. Reaches heights of up to 2 feet.

Phyllitis scolopendrium (hart's tongue fern) is evergreen, with leathery, upright fronds reaching heights of about 12-16 inches.

Osmunda regalis (royal fern) is a hardy deciduous fern which thrives in damp, shady locations. In autumn the foliage turns an attractive red-brown. It grows up to about 2-3 feet in height.

Matteuccia struthiopteris (ostrich fern) is an upright, deciduous fern, which—as its common name suggests—is shaped like a shuttlecock. It reaches a height of approximately 4 feet.

MAINTENANCE

Mulch the beds each spring with leaf compost or woodchip mulch.

Regularly weed the beds to prevent any of them taking over and smothering out the ferns.

The foliage of the deciduous ferns can be cut back once they have died back, although you don't need to worry about keeping it too tidy to keep the beds looking natural.

Tree ferns may need their crowns (at the top where the fronds emerge) to be protected with a frost cloth over winter in areas prone to frost.

FERNS

1 | *Phyllitis scolopendrium* (hart's tongue fern) ▫ **2** | *Dryopteris erythrosora* (Japanese shield fern)

▫ **3** | *Dicksonia antarctica* (tree fern) **4** | *Adiantum pedatum* (maidenhair fern) ▫ **5** | *Polystichum setiferum* (soft shield fern)

6 | *Osmunda regalis* (royal fern) ▫ **7** | *Matteuccia struthiopteris* (ostrich fern)

Planting project:
RAISED BEDS FOR SHADE

There are various reasons for shade in the garden. Sometimes it is solid, immovable objects such as buildings, structures, walls, and fences. Other times it can be the shade of a tree and other times it can just be the north-easterly aspect of the garden.

Although most people crave a sunny south-facing garden, there are plenty of shade-loving plants that will transform your outdoor space into a horticultural paradise. The main period of interest with shade-loving plants, such as bluebells, erythronium, and *Anemone blanda*, is often in spring because in nature this is before the overhead woodland canopy starts producing its foliage and casts its shade over the ground. However, there are other periods of flowering interest: plants such as fuchsias, saxifrage, and hosta flower during summer. Shade plants also offer fantastic opportunities for architectural structure and foliage, such as the shrub *Hydrangea quercifolia*, the holly, and the ground cover epimedium. Of course there are also lots of ferns that can be used in shady gardens (see ferns and stumperies, page 142).

Because the garden is in the shade, a timber raised bed will deteriorate at a quicker rate as it will be damper than a bed in full sun. It may therefore be worth considering brick raised beds, although using logs and lengths of trunks do give an attractive woodland feature to the shade garden.

PLANTING SUGGESTIONS:

- *Hosta* 'Big Daddy' (hosta) x 2
- *Epimedium grandiflorum* 'Lilafee' (bishop's hat) x 3
- *Saxifraga fortunei* (fortune saxifrage) x 1
- *Hyacinthoides non-scripta* (English bluebells) x 10
- *Hydrangea quercifolia* (oakleaf hydrangea) x 1
- *Ilex aquifolium* 'Silver Queen' x 1 (variegated holly)
- *Skimmia japonica* (skimmia) x 1
- *Anemone blanda* (winter windflower) x 3

1 | Fill up the raised bed with a mix of leaf compost and soil. Leaf compost is used because many of the shade-loving plants originate in the woodland, where they thrive in the rotted leaf litter from the deciduous trees. If you don't have leaf compost, you can make it by collecting up leaves and leaving them to rot for a year. It might not be ready in time for planting but it is useful for topping off the soil each year in the raised bed.

2 | Plant the shrubs, the hydrangea, holly, and skimmia, toward the back of the raised bed if it isn't possible to walk all the way around it. If it is, then plant them toward the center, where they will be shown off.

3 | Plant the hosta and saxifrage in front of the shrubs.

4 | Find a corner toward the front and plant the epimedium to grow and cover the ground.

5 | Plant the bulbs (anemone and bluebells) in among the other plants. Don't plant them near the epimedium as it will quickly swamp them. Choose native or English bluebells and avoid the hybrid or Spanish ones which are more vigorous and lack the scent and delicateness.

6 | Mulch the bed with woodchip mulch to help suppress the weeds.

Maintenance

Watch out for slugs on the hostas and treat with nematodes, slug pellets, or create a beer trap to prevent them from munching through the foliage of the plants. Put these in place just as the hostas emerge. When the plants are larger they should be OK.

If the shrubs get too big they will need pruning back to keep them in shape and prevent them taking over the rest of the border.

The epimedium could also take over the bed if allowed. Prune it back if necessary.

Top the bed up with leaf compost each spring and mulch with more woodchip mulch

CREATING A RAISED LAWN FOCAL POINT

This design is a simple raised bed featuring just turf on the surface with a gap in the center to plant a tree. Having a turf raised bed is a great solution for small gardens where you crave your own patch of lawn to sit, or even lie on, yet have concrete or paved floors. Creating a lawn on a raised bed makes it more comfortable for getting up from than the ground, which is very useful if a person has mobility issues.

A focal point

Having a small tree in the center creates an attractive focal point. Try to choose a tree with more than one season of interest such as an apple tree that produces blossom in spring and fruit in summer. *Cornus kousa* is a great tree for all-year-round interest, with attractive white flower bracts in spring, fruit in autumn, and an attractive looking trunk all year round. Other trees that could feature include an ornamental weeping pear or cherry tree. Avoid trees that will get too large, such as oak and beech.

How to create your raised lawn

For this project you are essentially making two frames for the raised bed: one slightly smaller, which will fit inside the other, creating a shape a bit like a square doughnut, leaving you with a hole in the middle for the tree to be planted.

1 | Create a wooden frame out of railroad ties (as seen on page 115) up to a height of about 20 inches.

2 | Create a smaller frame to fit inside this one, but to the same height. This frame should be built so there is about a 20 inch by 20 inch gap in the center where the tree will be planted.

3 | Dig over the ground in both areas of the raised bed. This will break up any compaction in the space between the raised bed and the area where the tree will be planted.

4 | Next plant your tree directly in the ground in the center. It may need a vertical stake with a tree tie to stop it hitting the sides of the raised bed in windy conditions.

5 | Water the tree in well.

6 | Fill the space between the two wooden frames with soil. You are now ready for either sowing grass seed or laying turf.

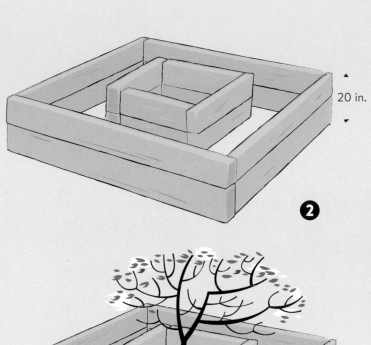

20 in.

2

4

6

Sowing grass seed or laying sod

Sowing grass seed is a much cheaper option but it will take longer to establish. Also, it is necessary to weed it while waiting for the seed to emerge and birds can eat the seed if it is not protected with a net. There is usually a better choice of types of grass seed available to buy than is offered with sod.

Laying sod creates an instant effect, although you will have to wait a week or two before using it to sit on. It is more expensive than seed, but it is easier to lay sod than sow a lawn. Sod can be laid all year round, but extremes of weather such as drought or snow should be avoided. Seed can only be sown when temperatures are above about 55 degrees Fahrenheit, depending on variety.

1 | This differs to most raised beds in that you want your soil in your raised bed to be flush with the top of the raised bed.

2 | Break the soil down to a fine tilth with a rake and make sure it is level.

3 | If you are sowing seed, then you need to sprinkle about a handful per square yard. You can mark it out with string if you're not sure. Then rake the seed lightly into the soil, water and cover with a net until germination. It will take between two and four weeks to germinate, but avoid doing this in the winter as it's too cold. Fall is a good time to sow grass seed.

4 | When laying sod, start on the edge and lay the pieces next to each other end to end leaving no gaps between. Firm each one down with the back of the rake. Stagger each row, like brickwork, and avoid walking over your raised bed for a week or two until the sod pieces have rooted.

MAINTENANCE

The lawn will need cutting once a week, but a very light cut with a good pair of sharp shears, will make light work of it. You will also want to edge it with a pair of edging shears to prevent it getting straggly at the sides.

Keep an eye on the edges of the lawn as it may dry out. Water it if it looks like it is starting to turn brown.

Dig out daisies and dandelions when they appear in the lawn to prevent them spreading and taking over.

The tree in the center should be maintained with a clean stem (or trunk) to prevent branches from lying across the turf and damaging it. Each year use a pair of pruners to remove any shoots along the lower section of the trunk or any suckering shoots that emerge from the roots, and when it's tall enough lift the crown of the tree to above head height.

Planting project:
PRAIRIE DESIGN

Prairie planting is influenced by the plains of North America and its main principles are drifts or blocks of herbaceous plants, movement and texture created by ornamental grasses, and long seasons of interest, whether it is from the flowers, seed heads in winter, or the foliage.

Originally this style was designed for large, long borders in grand gardens and public parks, but it is possible to replicate the style in smaller gardens and in raised beds. Choose a site in the sun. Prairie style gardening is low maintenance and will attract lots of wildlife to the garden.

Prairie plants can be grown in any type of raised bed, but because of their model style you could try growing them in shiny metal trough to give that chic feel to the garden. This bed suits a long raised bed where the plants are designed in drifts of color. For maximum effect have two long borders opposite each other and plant the blocks of plants slightly diagonally from each other so that it feels like they naturally drift from one side to another. Walking between the two raised beds full of these impressive and elaborate plants combining movement, texture, and color is a magical experience.

PLANTING SUGGESTIONS:

Here are the plants you will need (double the amount if planting two parallel raised beds) for a border measuring 20 feet long by 3 feet wide. The color palette is a muted yellow, with each block of flowering plants interspersed with the impressive ornamental grass *Stipa tenuissima*, with its appealing pale yellow effect.

- *Stipa tenuissima* (Mexican feather grass) x 9
- *Achillea filipendulina* 'Gold Plate' (yarrow) x 3
- *Echinacea paradoxa* (Bush's purple coneflower) x 3
- *Phlomis russeliana* (Turkish sage) x 3

1 | Fill the raised bed with a mix of soil and compost and rake it level to just below the height of the raised bed.
2 | Starting at the nearest edge, plant a block of three stipa plants in a slight diagonal angle across the bed. If you're doing a double border, then continue the diagonal line with three more grasses.
3 | Three feet along the border plant the three achillea at a parallel diagonal angle to the stipa. Continue the diagonal across on the other side of the border.
4 | Repeat the process at the next yard marker with three more stipa, followed by three *Echinacea paradoxa*, three more grasses, and finally the three *Phlomis russeliana*.
5 | Water the plants in well. The plants will soon grow and fill in the bare spaces, making it feel like a vibrant and flamboyant border full of movement and color.
6 | Mulch the borders with gravel to help suppress weeds.

Yarrow

Coneflower

Phlomis

Feather grass

Maintenance

None of the plants should need staking as the surrounding plants should prop each other up. Allow the plants to flop and spill over the edge as this adds to the prairie feel.

Resist cutting back the herbaceous plants in autumn as the seed heads should still provide an impressive display in winter, particularly when they get caught by the frosts. Also the birds will appreciate the additional winter supply of seed and nesting material. Instead, cut the herbaceous plants back in early spring, as the new growth is just beginning to emerge.

(You can plant bulbs in autumn, which will give some interest after the display is cut back in early spring.)

Top off the gravel mulch every couple of years.

The herbaceous plants may need dividing every three years if they are getting too large for their location. Throw away the older, central parts of the plant and replant with three young, fresh sections for each block.

MINI WILDFLOWER MEADOW BORDER

If you want to bring a bit of the countryside into your garden at home, then creating a wildflower meadow in a raised bed could be the answer. They are very easy to create, and the cost is minimal, literally just the price of a packet of seeds. Wildflower meadows will attract bees, butterflies, and birds into the garden, making it a haven for wildlife.

Wildflower requirements

Most wildflower meadows prefer light, infertile soil as fertility leads to competition with coarse grasses and vigorous weeds which can take over. Ensure that the soil in the raised beds is weed free to begin with. Using good-quality screened topsoil would be one way to do this. There are lots of different types of mixes to try from seed companies—some are themed by colors such as "strawberries and cream," which features red and white wildflowers; others are designed to give you a period of interest for as long as possible. Wildflower seed should be sown between mid spring and early summer. The earlier you sow the seed, the longer you will have to enjoy the floral display.

MAINTENANCE

The great feature of wildflower meadows is that they are low maintenance. Once the seed has been sown there is very little to do to maintain them. They don't require staking, and they are fairly drought tolerant so shouldn't need watering unless in an extreme period of drought.

The wildflowers should be cut back to near ground level once they have finished flowering and set seed. On a small area a pair of shears can be used, but in larger raised beds a string trimmer could be used. Shake the seed heads onto the soil to ensure they flower again next year. Alternatively collect the seed into paper bags and store in a dry, frost-free place, ready to sow again next year.

How to create your mini meadow

Any type of raised bed can be used, but they look most effective in rustic looking designs such as willow woven beds or chunky railroad ties.

1 | Fill the top 4 inches of your raised bed with a 50:50 mix of topsoil and sand. The sand provides added drainage and is low in fertility, which most (but not all) wild flowers prefer.

2 | Use a rake to break the soil down to a fine tilth and then rake it level, leaving it about 20 inches below the top of the raised bed.

3 | Open up the packet of wildflower seeds and sow it following the sowing rate guidelines. This is usually explained as

a rate per square foot. You can mark out an area in the bed with string and sow accordingly.

4 | When sowing, it is a good idea to sow half of the mix in one direction, and then the other half at 90 degrees to it. This should ensure an equal distribution of the seeds.

5 | After sowing, the seeds can be very lightly raked in to ensure they are just under the surface of the soil. Water the bed and then cover with a net to prevent birds from eating the seeds.

6 | Remove the net once the seeds have germinated.

Planting project:
HARDY ANNUALS

The cheapest way to grow plants is to sow annuals from seed. For hardly any money at all, literally the price of a few packets of seeds, you can have a fantastic display of bright, colorful flowers.

Annuals couldn't be simpler to grow and once they germinate there is very little maintenance required—just leave them to do their thing, which is flowering their hearts out all summer long.

In this planting design only the sweet peas and sunflowers need to be grown in pots first before planting out. The other plants listed just need to be scattered onto the soil and raked in during spring. It couldn't be easier.

Hardy annuals tend to suit the rustic, cottage garden look, so bear this in mind when deciding what type of raised bed to grow them in. They'll look good in chunky timber or woven willow. Recycled bricks will also add charm to the planting scheme. Most hardy annuals prefer to be grown in full sun in well-drained soil. Add plenty of organic matter to the soil. These annuals need to make all their growth, flower and seeds in one season, so they need as big a boost as they can get once they start germinating.

PLANTING SUGGESTIONS:

- *Lathyrys* (sweet peas)
- *Helianthus* (sunflowers)
- *Centaurea cyanus* (cornflower)
- *Calendula officinalis* (pot marigold)
- *Limnanthes douglasii* (poached egg flower)
- *Lunaria annua* (honesty)
- *Nigella damascena* (love-in-a-mist)
- *Consolida* (larkspur)
- *Papaver commutatum, P. rhoeas, P. somniferum* (corn and opium poppies)

Sunflowers come in a variety of heights, colors, and flower types (single and double). Sow a mixture for a more interesting display.

1 | In the center of the raised bed create a teepee structure using 6 foot bamboo stakes. Space the stakes out equally in a 1 yard-diameter circle. Lean all the stakes inwards and tie them together with garden twine at the top.

2 | Place two sweet pea seedlings at the base of each stake. Lean the plant toward the structure. This will encourage its tendrils to reach up and attach to the stakes as it starts to grow. The sweet peas can be grown earlier in autumn, by sowing a seed in small pots in general compost and keeping it on a windowsill or in a greenhouse over winter. Plant them out in spring.

3 | The giant sunflowers can be planted toward the back of the raised bed. Space them 12 inches apart and place a stake next to each one for them to grow up. The sunflowers can be sown in small plastic pots in seedling mix in spring and planted out when they are between 4-8 inches tall. Alternatively, they can be sown directly in the soil where they are to be grown.

4 | With the remainder of the hardy annual seeds use sand to create patterns on the surface of the soil and then sprinkle the packets of seeds into them. Rake them gently into the soil and water using a watering can with a breaker attachment.

5 | It may be necessary to protect newly sown seeds from birds by placing a net over the raised bed until they have germinated.

Cornflower · Sweet pea · Sunflower · Poppy · Love-in-a-mist · Honesty · Poached egg flower · Larkspur · Marigold

Maintenance

Water the plants in dry periods and keep the raised beds weed free by regularly hoeing out annual weeds as soon as they appear, being careful not to damage the emerging seedlings.

Keep picking the sweet peas to ensure they flower all summer long. Deadhead the annuals so that they continue to bloom.

The sunflowers will need tying to the supporting stakes as they continue to grow. Leave the flower head in situ once it starts to fade as birds will feed on the seeds.

Planting project:
WINTER BEDDING

When most people think of bedding plants they think of bright spring and summer displays. However, there are plenty of plants suitable to create a bedding display in winter that will brighten the dullest and coldest of days.

Bedding plants are usually low-growing plants. Planting them in a raised bed lifts them closer to eye level, increasing your enjoyment of them. Bedding plants are usually used as temporary displays and normally removed and added to the compost heap after flowering. Although they can be raised from seed, they can easily be bought in bulk as plug plants for reasonably small amounts of money, which saves time—also helpful if you don't have a greenhouse for raising seedlings.

Bedding plants were very popular in Victorian times. The key feature is the patterns that are created using the flowers and the foliage. As a rule of thumb, with bedding plants, usually the brighter the better. And the more garish and outlandish the color scheme, the more visual impact it has. However, if you prefer softer colors, then select bedding plant varieties with pastel colors. If you can't find the plants specified, select bedding plants that are seasonally available in your area.

If you only have one raised bed, which is already planted with herbaceous perennials, then winter bedding can be planted among the existing scheme as the perennial plants die back over winter. The suggested scheme in this planting project assumes that the entire bed is empty.

PLANTING SUGGESTIONS:

- **Outside edges:** bellis, aubretia, and polyanthus
- **Filler plants:** erysimum (wallflowers), winter pansies, cyclamen, winter-flowering heather, bergenias, and heuchera
- **Interplants:** flowering cabbage and kale, tulips, hyacinths, and daffodils
- **Dot plants:** cordyline, phormium, topiary, or standard bay

1 | Fill up the raised bed with a 50:50 mix of compost and topsoil. Mound the soil so that it is slightly higher in the center of the bed. This helps to show off the plants.

2 | Prior to planting, it is best to draw out a plan of the pattern intended. This will also help in deciding how many plants to buy. Once drawn up, use string or sand to mark out where the plants are going to go.

3 | Around the outside edges of the beds plant bedding such as bellis, aubretia, and polyanthus. Plant them 6 inches apart. These define the structure of the bed and should be in formal, straight lines.

4 | The bulk of the planting and color scheme will be made up with filler, or groundwork, plants. They should be planted 10 inches apart. Bedding plants suitable include erysimum (wallflowers), winter pansies, cyclamen, winter-flowering heather, bergenias, and heuchera.

5 | Interplants should be planted throughout the central section of the scheme and often include ornamental winter brassicas and hellebores. If you want to extend the season into spring, then also plant bulbs, such as tulips, hyacinths, and daffodils.

6 | Usually in most bedding planting schemes there are two or three dot plants that add height and focal features. Plants often include cordyline, phormium, and occasionally topiary or standard bay.

Aubretia
Polyanthus
Erysimum
Cyclamen
Heuchera
Tulips
Daffodils
Hyacinths
Cordyline
Phormium
Box
Bellis

Maintenance

Deadheading the flowers as they fade will help to encourage more to be produced.

Water the plants after planting. Because it is winter, they shouldn't really need watering again, except during elongated periods of dry weather.

After the period of flowering is over, many of the plants can be removed and thrown away. They can then be replaced with spring bedding such as primroses, primulas, and violas.

Dot plants such as cordyline, phormium, and any other shrubs can remain in position, as can the bulbs.

MINI APPLE ORCHARD

Apple trees can be grown in the tiniest of spaces. A small sheltered spot in full sun will provide plenty of fruit and the trees will make an attractive feature in the garden. Growing a mini fruit orchard in a raised bed helps to give an area of the garden definition and makes a feature of the trees.

Why apple trees?

Apple trees don't just provide delicious, juicy, and colorful fruit, there are many other benefits to growing them too. They will attract wildlife into the garden, they provide a flowering display of blossom in spring that is just as good as any ornamental tree, and as they mature they form impressive gnarly trunks that provide an additional period of interest in winter. There are over a thousand apple varieties to choose from, ranging from tiny yellow fruits to huge red apple varieties. By choosing different varieties you can ensure that you have apples to eat from late summer to late winter.

Size matters

The size of the tree is determined by the type of rootstock that it has been grafted or budded onto. Garden centers and nurseries can advise you, but you need to ask for fruit trees on "dwarfing" rootstock as this will ensure trees won't get any taller than about 5-8 feet. Around the edge of the raised bed are "stepover" apples, so called because they are low enough to step over, although possibly not on the raised bed.

Selecting your varieties

This raised bed is 12 feet by 12 feet, and it is amazing how many trees can be squeezed into such a tiny space. In this raised bed you could fit four freestanding apple trees in the center of the bed and then ten stepover trees around the edge. Suggestions for the four free standing trees are 'Discovery' (early), 'James Grieve' (mid), 'Egremont Russet' (mid to late) and 'Edward VII'. The first three varieties are dessert varieties and will provide fruit from late summer through to winter if Egremont Russet is stored after picking in a frost-free, dry location. Edward VII is a cooking type that is perfect for making apple pies, crumbles, or sauce. The stepover trees around the outside can be any variety you like, to complement the four central trees.

Try to pick a range of different colors, sizes and harvest times to create interest in the bed. Select fruit trees from similar pollination groups, so that they will flower at around the same time. This will mean that bees and other pollinating insects pass on the pollen from one tree to another, which should ensure a good crop of fruit. If you are unsure about pollination groups, then the garden center or nursery you procure the plants from should be able to advise you. It's important to select varieties that will grow well in your area so that you end up with a big harvest!

MAINTENANCE

Once established the trees around the edge of the bed need to be pruned twice a year: first in late summer where their new growth should be pruned back to two buds, and second in winter when the clusters of fruit bud spurs should be thinned out to leave groups of about four of five buds.

As the fruits develop in summer, they should be thinned out to leave just one or two per cluster. This is to ensure that the remaining fruits develop to their full size.

The trees in the middle of the bed should be pruned in winter, removing any crossing branches and ensuring that branches will receive enough sunlight in summer to ripen the fruit.

How to create your mini apple orchard

Choose a low type of raised bed such as a single tier of gravel boards as this will make it easy to get onto the beds to maintain the trees and harvest the fruit. The best time to plant an apple tree is in autumn when the soil is still warm but there is enough time for the roots to establish before winter, but they can be planted at any time of year, avoiding extremes of weather such as drought or harsh frosts.

1 | Build a raised bed measuring 12 feet by 12 feet from gravel boards (as shown on page 89) and dig the soil beneath the area of the bed to a depth of one spade to ensure that the roots of the tree will be able to grow downwards. The plants should have a dwarfing rootstock, and they will also need to be pruned so that they do not spread too much and start to grow into one another.

2 | Add soil to the raised bed so that it is just below the level of the top of the gravel board.

3 | Put in four 6 foot upright posts 3 feet apart in the center of the bed. These will be the stakes that support the free-standing apple trees.

4 | Dig out planting holes at the base of each post. Plant the trees ensuring that the graft union (the knobby bit near the base of the trunk) is above the soil. Use a tree tie to attach the tree to the post.

5| Bang 2 foot tall posts in each corner of the raised bed and stretch a wire between each post, running parallel with the edge of the bed. The posts should be about 12 inches away from the edge of the bed.

6| Plant the stepover apple trees at a spacing of 3 feet between each tree and prune the trunk so that it is just below the height of the wire. This should encourage a couple of branches to grow, one which should be trained along the wire in one direction and the other branch in the opposite direction.

Planting project:
WINTER GARDEN

There is no reason why a garden shouldn't look just as great in winter as in summer. There is a plethora of winter-flowering trees and shrubs that look beautiful, as well as herbaceous plants and bulbs.

Evergreen shrubs add structure and texture in winter, while other plants, such as yew, skimmia, holly, and ivy, produce attractive berries. Finally, there are attractive, colorful winter stems such as willow and dogwood.

Position your raised bed near the house and you can admire your winter garden from the warmth and comfort of your home. However, even better is to step outside, as many of the winter plants have flowers that fragrance the cool winter air with their exquisite perfume—another good reason to have the raised bed positioned near a door or path that gets used a lot in winter so that you can regularly enjoy the perfume. If your raised bed has a fence or wall at the back then you could consider growing attractive colorful climbers at the back such as variegated ivies.

This specific raised bed project may not be suited for every climate region. Make sure you select plants that will thrive during the winters in your region.

PLANTING SUGGESTIONS:

- *Sarcococca hookeriana* var. *digyna* (sweet box) x 1
- *Chimonanthus praecox* (wintersweet) x 1
- *Eranthis hyemalis* (winter aconite) x 100
- *Hamamelis mollis* (witch hazel) x 1
- *Cornus sanguinea* 'Midwinter Fire' (dogwood) x 3
- *Galanthus nivalis* (common snowdrop) x 100
- *Hedera helix* 'Goldheart' (variegated ivy) x 1

1 | If the raised bed is less than a foot and a half tall then the soil below the raised bed will need digging over to break up any compaction. This is because many of the shrubs in this design will need the space for their roots to reach down into.

2 | Fill up the flower bed with a 50:50 mix of compost and soil to just below the top of the raised bed.

3 | Space out the shrubs with the fragrant winter flowers (hamamelis, chimonanthus, and sarcococca), as these form the backbone so that they feel balanced in the raised bed.

4 | Plant out the three cornus (dogwoods) closely together in a group (about 2 feet apart) to maximize the impact that their winter stems will have.

5 | In between the shrubs plant the bulbs (galanthus, or snowdrops, and winter aconites). These will provide a colorful white and yellow carpet in winter and act as a wonderful backdrop to the shrubs.

6 | Water the plants in thoroughly, and then cover any bare soil with a woodchip or bark mulch.

7 | If there is a wall or fence at the back then the ivy can be trained up the wall for an additional splash of bright winter color.

The circular diagram is divided into wedges, each labeled with a plant name:
- Wintersweet
- Sweet box
- Dogwood
- Variegated ivy
- Winter aconite
- Witch hazel
- Snowdrop

Maintenance

The winter scented shrubs (hamamelis, chimonanthus, and sarcococca) will occasionally need pruning back if they get too large for their position.

The cornus (dogwood) should be cut back to near ground level in early spring. This ensures that you get the maximum amount of time to enjoy the brightly colored winter stems.

Regularly weed the beds to ensure that the plants are free from competition for nutrients. Every couple of years the bed should be topped off with woodchip or bark mulch.

RAISED KNOT GARDEN

Knot gardens were first created in medieval times, particularly in monastic gardens, but are enjoying a revival. The design involves creating patterns in among the planting using evergreen planting, focusing on texture and foliage. Herbs are usually planted in between the structural, evergreen patterns, but it can be any type of plant. Patterns can be intricate or simple, depending on the design.

Plant varieties

Box (*Buxus sempervirens*) is the traditional plant used to create the structure of the knot garden, and there are variations if you wish to put a twist on the design, such as golden-leafed and variegated forms. However, due to the prevalence of box blight, which kills the plant, modern designs often use alternative evergreen shrubs that look similar to box. Good alternatives for structure include:

- *Ilex crenata*
- *Berberis buxifolia* 'Pygmaea'
- *Lonicera nitida*

The herbs rosemary or lavender can also be used as an alternative to box.

Create a focal point

Knot gardens always look best when there is a focal point in the center of the design. Features that can look good include sculptures, birdbaths, or sundials. Impressive topiaries also look good as a central feature or an evergreen plant such as a standard bay tree or an olive tree in a pot.

MAINTENANCE

Box should be pruned after the risk of frost is over. Use a pair of hand shears to prune back the new growth. Clip back tight each year, or twice a year, to ensure that the parterre pattern is kept well defined and within bounds. Use a string to ensure you keep a straight line. Eventually the box plants should grow or knit together to make it look like one seamless hedge.

- Trim the herbs at the end of the season to keep them looking tidy.

- The box plants will need watering when they're young during dry periods in the summer.

- Regularly weed between the plants to prevent them from taking over and spreading in the bed.

How to create your knot garden

It is best to keep the design simple for a knot garden in a small space, because anything too intricate will look messy and complicated. This design simply features box plants around the edge of the bed and then two diagonal lines going from corner to corner. In the center is a small circle of box which surrounds the focal point, an olive tree in a pot.

1 | Plant box plants around the edge of the raised bed, spacing the plants at 12 inches apart.

2 | Use a string as a guideline stretching diagonally from corner to corner and plant box plants at 12 inch intervals. Leave a 2 foot gap in the center of the bed on each diagonal.

3 | Create a circle of box in the gap in the center of the bed.

4 | Create a plinth in the center of the bed. A patio slab or a few level bricks should suffice.

5 | Place your central feature on the plinth, in this case an olive tree in a terracotta pot.

6 | Fill the four quarters between the box diagonals with plants. A suggested planting scheme could be four textural plants, with lavender, Santolina chamaecyparissus (cotton lavender), rosemary, and Helichrysum italicum (curry plant).

7 | Mulch the soil with a thin layer of gravel. This will, to some extent, reduce the chance of weeds germinating and will look attractive. If you want to be creative you can use different color gravels for each corner to add an extra dimension of interest.

Planting project:

COTTAGE GARDEN RAISED BED

Nothing encompasses the romance and beauty of an outdoor space better than a cottage garden packed full of large, flowering plants with drifts of herbaceous perennials, jostling for position among rambling roses and shrubs.

The cottage garden style avoids symmetry and formal rows of plants. Instead, the focus is on making the planting feel natural, as if nature rather than a gardener is at work. Cottage garden perennial plants are perfect in a raised bed as they don't require the large root run and depth of soil that trees and shrubs may need. In addition, the extra height shows off their impressive flowers better than if they were grown directly in the ground.

There are a whole range of cottage garden plants to choose from, but listed right are some examples of commonly found ones. Ideally the bed should be created in full sun, which is where these plants do best, although they will tolerate some dappled shade.

PLANTING SUGGESTIONS:

- *Delphinium* 'Black Knight' (delphinium)
- *Allium hollandicum* 'Purple Sensation' (flowering onion)
- *Echinacea purpurea* (purple coneflower)
- *Foeniculum vulgare* 'Purpureum' (bronze fennel)
- *Rudbeckia fulgida* var. *sullivantii* 'Goldsturm' (black-eyed Susan)
- *Geranium* 'Johnson's Blue' (geranium)

1 | Create a raised bed from natural, rustic looking material such as recycled lumber, logs, or railroad ties. Old recycled bricks could work equally well.

2 | Fill the beds up with a mix of 50:50 topsoil and garden compost.

3 | Plant the delphiniums at the back of the border where their tall, stately, dark blue flower spikes will make an impressive backdrop.

4 | The allium bulbs should be planted to a depth of at least double their size. The stunning round purple flower heads will grow to about 3 feet tall.

5 | At the front of the bed plant the geranium and let the flowers and foliage trail over the edge of the raised bed.

6 | The fennel (foeniculum) has attractive fern-like foliage and makes a nice contrast if planted just in front of the dark blue delphiniums.

7 | Plant the echinacea and rudbeckia toward the middle of the bed in drifts. The golden splash of rudbeckia will make an attractive contrast to the blues and purples of the other plants.

Delphinium

Flowering onion

Coneflower

Geranium

Fennel

Coneflower

Maintenance

The delphinium flower spikes will need staking to prevent them from breaking. After flowering the spike can be cut back to encourage new ones to grow.

Keep the beds free from weeds and water the plants regularly after planting during spring and summer.

Cut back the herbaceous perennials to near ground level after flowering.

After a few years, some of the herbaceous perennials may need dividing if they have outgrown their location.

To extend the flowering season, half of the echinacea and rudbeckia can be chopped back in mid spring so the uncut plants flower first, and the cut ones flower a few weeks later.

GOURMET VEGETABLE GARDEN

The majority of gardeners with raised beds use them for growing vegetables in. However, if you only have a small garden then you will be limited to how many vegetables you can grow. One of the advantages of growing your own food is that you have a wider range of plants to choose from than those to be found in the supermarket or greengrocer's. The raised bed below suggests some gourmet vegetables that are easy to grow, yet not readily available in the shops. There are loads of other delicious vegetables worth trying, so the best thing is to experiment yourself, growing vegetables that you personally like and that you find fun to grow.

Carrots: Although carrots are easy to find in the shop, there are some more quirky, unusual varieties that are not often found. The small globe carrots 'Parmex' taste sweet and are great eaten either raw in salads or added to stews and casseroles. There are also purple and yellow carrots worth trying, such as 'Purple Haze' or 'Yellowstone'.

Sow carrots into shallow rows just $^1/_4$ inch deep directly into the soil and water them in well. Thin the seedlings out when they get to about 3 inches tall to leave 3 inches between each plant.

Potatoes: These are cheap to buy and readily available but there are a few varieties that you can't buy for love or money. Try 'Salad Blue', which produce blue potatoes that retain their color after cooking, or 'Burgundy Red' for red ones.

Potatoes should be planted in springtime in a trench about 10 inches deep and about 4 inches apart. Backfill with a mix of compost and soil. Potatoes are ready after the plants have flowered. Use a fork to dig them out of the ground. For a small raised bed it is probably only worth growing about five tubers so as not to take up too much space.

Courgettes: Courgettes can be pricey to buy in the shops yet one or two plants will produce bumper crops each year. And choose some of the more interesting colors and flavors such as white, black, or yellow varieties.

Courgettes need to be planted in individual pots from mid to late spring. Place the seed on its side so that it doesn't rot. Plant them out in the raised bed after the risk of frost is over, because they are tender. Add plenty of organic matter to the planting hole prior to planting as they are hungry plants. Keep them well watered and feed them once a week with a liquid fertilizer. A raised bed will only need one or two plants as they should produce bumper crops that will easily be enough to feed a family throughout summer.

Salad leaves: Lettuces can easily be bought from the shops, but there are lots of interesting salad leaves that are easy to grow, such as rocket, mizuna, radicchio, and lots of cut-and-come-again salads, worth trying.

Salad leaves can be sown directly into the soil in shallow rows in raised beds. Sow in spring and keep them watered. Most can be cut to near ground level with scissors and they should regrow new leaves, ready for harvesting a few weeks later. Regularly sow every few weeks to ensure there are always plenty of leaves to harvest.

Beans and peas: There are lots of colorful beans and peas, such as 'Purple Teepee' French bean and the purple mangetout 'Shiraz'.

Peas can be sown directly in the soil from early spring. Plant them about 6 inches apart and push in pea sticks for them to clamber up. Beans can be sown in pots from mid to late spring. Plant them out after the risk of frost is over. Dwarf varieties can be chosen to make harvesting easier from a raised bed.

Tomatoes: There's a huge range of exciting and colorful tomatoes to try, such as the huge beefsteak variety called 'Black Russian' or the small yellow 'Golden Sweet'.

The best time to sow tomatoes is early spring. Alternatively, buy young plants, as there is an increasing range of unusual types available now as seedlings. Sow them in individual pots indoors and keep them on a windowsill or in a greenhouse until the risk of frost is over. Then plant them out in a sheltered, warm area of the raised bed. They will need supporting with stakes or cages to train them up. Give them a liquid feed with tomato fertilizer once a week once they start to form flowers.

Brussels sprouts: If you can't bear the thought of sprouts at the Christmas dinner then there are sweeter varieties you could try growing in your garden, such as 'Trafalagar' or kale/sprout crosses that aren't so bitter.

Sprouts can be sown in spring in individual pots. Once the seedlings are about 4 inches tall they can be planted in the raised bed. Plant them in rows and add lots of organic matter such as garden compost or manure to the soil as they are hungry plants. Once they start to form sprouts they may need supporting with a stake to prevent them blowing over. Sprouts can be harvested in autumn and winter.

Planting project:
SOFT FRUIT GARDEN

Soft fruits provide a colorful display of berries throughout summer as well as supplying delicious flavored home-grown fruit to either eat fresh or cook in the kitchen.

Raspberries

Strawberries

Grapes

Gooseberries

Blackcurrants

Redcurrants

Soft fruit is easy to grow and anyone who has tasted home-grown strawberries and raspberries would agree that nothing tasting anywhere near as good can be bought from the shops. Soft fruit doesn't take up much space and is therefore perfect for growing in small gardens and in raised beds.

Gooseberries and redcurrants can be grown in shade or partially shaded areas of the raised bed. All the other fruit bushes should ideally be grown in full sun for them to ripen fully and develop their sweet flavors. The plants will need a fairly deep root run, so if the raised bed is shallow, the soil beneath the bed should be dug over and organic matter added.

Maintenance

The raspberries should have their old canes cut back after they have fruited in late summer, and the new canes which will bear the fruit next year should be tied in.

The blackcurrants should be pruned in winter. Remove about a third of the old stems near the base.

Gooseberries and redcurrants can be pruned in exactly the same way. Create an open centered bush, pruning back any stems growing into the center. Cut back new wood on the existing framework back to two buds.

Blackcurrants, redcurrants, and gooseberries will also benefit from a summer prune by cutting new growth back to five leaves. This allows the sunlight into the center of the bush which helps to ripen the fruit, but also helps to prevent a build-up of humidity within the canopy which can cause fungal diseases such as mildew.

Strawberries will need straw placed under the fruit as they start to ripen to prevent them rotting. Strawberry plants should be replaced every two or three years with new ones. Keep an eye out for slugs, which love the ripening fruit.

Continue to train the grapevine up the arch. Cut the remaining new growth or laterals each summer back to five leaves and to two buds in winter.

Birds love eating freshly grown soft fruit, so the plants should be covered with a net as the fruit starts to ripen. It is worth considering a walk-in fruit cage to protect them.

PLANTING SUGGESTIONS:

- Raspberry plants x 10
- Strawberry plants x 15
- Gooseberry plants x 2
- Redcurrant plants x 2
- Blackcurrant plants x 2
- Grapevine x 1

1 | The summer fruiting raspberries require a training system to grow the canes up onto. Bang in two posts 10 feet apart and stretch two horizontal wires between them, one at 20 inches high and one at 4 feet high. Plant the raspberries 8-12 inches apart.

2 | The gooseberries, redcurrants, and blackcurrants should be planted 3 feet apart in the raised bed. The blackcurrants should be planted deeper than they were in the pot, whereas the redcurrants and gooseberries should be planted at the same depth as they were in the pot.

3 | If there is a fence or wall at the back of the raised bed, then set up a system of trellis or wires and plant the grape at its base. If there isn't one, then consider erecting an arch in the center of the bed to create interest, and train the grape up and over this.

4 | Finally, plant strawberries along the edge of the bed.

5 | Water the plants well and mulch around the base of the gooseberries, redcurrants, blackcurrants, and grapevine with well-rotted manure or compost. The raspberries could also be mulched, taking care not to have any of the material in contact with the canes as this will cause them to rot.

PERSONALIZING YOUR RAISED BED

Gardening can be a bit like interior decorating sometimes, whereby it is your opportunity to put your own personal stamp on an area, reflecting individual tastes or interests. Raised beds give a perfect opportunity to have a bit of fun and show a creative and artistic flourish that makes your garden stand out from the crowd. Of course, the choice of material the bed is made from, the type of plants chosen, and the style of design all reflect the owner's personality, but there are other things that can be done to make it more your own.

Gnomes and other statues

Some people have a penchant for garden gnomes and love to decorate their beds with these traditional Victorian garden features. Although they're not to everybody's taste, other forms of statues and ornaments can be used within raised beds. Whether it be cheap seaside artifacts brought back home as a souvenir of a lovely summer holiday or attractive Italian sculptures, they all add to the interest of the raised bed, particularly during winter when there might not be much other interest out there. Others may choose to place Lego ® or toy figures and characters from their favorite film or TV program among the beds. Woodcarvings can also make interesting features!

Decorating a raised bed

Raised beds can be made from bricks and breeze blocks which can then be rendered with cement and decorated by pushing pebbles into it while it is still wet. Seashells can make an attractive feature if living near a beach, or just simply if you want the sense of a coastal garden at home. Ceramic tiles can be used to create mosaics and patterns, giving the raised bed a sense of Mediterranean or North African culture.

Messages

Writing poetry or famous sayings on slate, wood, or pebbles is also a lovely way of personalizing a raised bed. They can make attractive features in their own right, and if put strategically among the bed they can be thought-provoking or inspiring when come across in the garden.

Planting project:

RAISED BED FOR CHILDREN

Although children are closer to plants anyway due to their height, a raised bed puts the plants right under their noses, which makes it even more enticing and interesting to them.

The trick with getting children interested in growing their own food is to make it fun and interactive, but more importantly, to choose food that they like to eat. Fruit is a popular choice, particularly strawberries, raspberries, blackberries, and blueberries. It's also great because the taste is instant. It doesn't have to be cooked, simply picked, washed, and eaten fresh, which is far more appealing to a hungry child than having to wait until it has been cooked in the kitchen. That said, making homemade French fries from home-grown potatoes makes the humble spud a popular choice for growing in a raised bed. Children love digging about in the raised bed to harvest the tubers. Other popular vegetables include cucumber, sweetcorn, snap peas, and sweet potatoes. Children also like a challenge, so consider encouraging them to grow a giant pumpkin or tall sunflower.

Gardening is a great way to get young children away from laptops and televisions and into the outdoors. It creates a healthier lifestyle and increases their knowledge of food.

Raised beds for children shouldn't be too high, as they won't be able to reach. The maximum height is probably 12 inches. You should also keep them small in terms of length and width. About 3 feet by 3 feet is ideal—any larger and the beds will start to become unmanageable and children will lose interest. Potatoes can be grown in rubber tires (see page 19) or compost bags.

PLANTING SUGGESTIONS:

1 | Create two or three raised beds, ensuring that they are not too high and that the children can comfortably reach into the center of the bed without having to climb onto it.

2 | Fill them up with topsoil or compost to just below the level of the top of the raised bed.

3 | In the center of one bed, create a small teepee out of willow sticks. At the base of the canes plant outside climbing cucumbers such as 'Crystal Apple'. These should be started by sowing one seed per pot in spring and planted outside once the risk of frost is over.

4 | In another bed you could consider growing cherry tomatoes. Sow seeds in late winter and keep indoors on a sunny window ledge or greenhouse. Plant out once the risk of frost has passed, at a distance of 1 foot (in a 3 foot-square bed that should be three rows with three plants in each). Rig up vertical bamboo stakes to support each stem and then run string between the stakes to support the fruiting branches.

5 | Strawberries can be grown in growbags on planks (see pages 110–111).

6 | Snap peas can be sown directly in the soil in shallow rows 4-6 inches apart within the rows and 10 inches between each row. Push in twiggy pea sticks next to the rows for the peas to cling onto with their tendrils as they grow.

7 | Sweetcorn should be sown in small pots indoors in late spring and then planted out once the risk of frost is over. Plant them in a grid system instead of rows, as they are pollinated by wind—pollen will be blown from one plant to another better if planted in a square pattern. Plant them 12 inches apart there should be room for nine plants in a 3 foot-square bed.

Sweetcorn

Strawberries

Cherry tomatoes

Snap peas

Cucumber

Maintenance

Give all the fruit and vegetable plants a balanced liquid feed every couple of weeks to keep them producing crops.

Keep the beds weed free, as it is unlikely the children will do it. But there is no harm in trying to encourage them.

Once the crops have been harvested they can be dug up and added to the compost heap. Dig organic matter into the beds the following spring in preparation for growing more vegetables the next year.

Planting project:

RAISED BED FOR BEES

Raised beds can be planted up with flowers that bees will love, encouraging these important pollinating insects into your garden.

There has been a decline in honeybees over recent years, thought to have been caused by a number of factors, including a lack of variety of plants, with intensive mono-culture farming. Gardeners have an opportunity to plant a wide range of plants that bees can forage on, which should hopefully help to prevent a further reduction in bee numbers.

There is nothing more relaxing than watching honeybees in the garden as they fly from plant to plant collecting pollen and nectar. Honeybees will travel over three miles to forage, so even if there isn't a beehive in your neighborhood they will still visit your raised bed if you fill it with the right kind of plants. Visiting bees will reward you with more flowers and increased fruit and vegetable yields as they will pollinate your crops.

If you really want to get serious about bees, you could consider a beehive in your garden. Even in a small space, if it is positioned correctly on the raised bed the bees should be able to fly back and forth to their hive without disturbing you. One of the tricks to avoid coming into contact with bees is to place the hive with the entrance hole of the hive away from the main pathways and seating areas in the garden, facing a wall or fence. This will cause the bees to fly up above head height as they leave the hive.

PLANTING SUGGESTIONS:

Here are some of the most common nectar- and pollen-rich plants worth growing:

☐ Bluebell	☐ Fennel	☐ Ivy
☐ Lavender	☐ Geranium	☐ Scabious
☐ Rosemary	☐ Verbascum	☐ Heather
☐ Fruit trees	☐ Potentilla	☐ Sedum
☐ Hawthorn	☐ Buddleja	☐ Yarrow
☐ Astilbe	☐ Cornflower	☐ Shasta daisy
☐ Comfrey	☐ Eryngium	☐ Purple
☐ Delphinium	☐ Fuchsia	coneflower

1 | Place the beehive at the farthest edge of the raised bed with the entrance facing toward a fence or wall. Alternatively, stretch a fine-gauged mesh in front of the entrance between two wooden posts. Make the mesh about 5 feet tall. This will force the bees to fly upwards and overhead.

2 | Avoid double-flowering plants as bees find them hard to access. Although bees mainly fly in spring and summer, they do forage in winter on mild days. So make sure there are plants that flower in all seasons.

3 | Bees like to forage from flower to flower, so plant in close clumps rather than singularly with lots of space between.

4 | If you have room in the raised bed, plant fruit trees on dwarf rootstocks. Bees love the pollen and nectar of fruit blossom.

5 | Place dishes of water for the bees to rest in and drink. Make sure the water dishes are shallow or filled with pebbles so that the bees don't fall in and drown.

Lavender

Geranium

Fuchsia

Buddleja

Maintenance

Keep the water dish topped off with water to continue enticing bees into the garden.

Avoid pesticides as some evidence has shown that it has a detrimental effect on bees' health.

Herbaceous perennials should be divided up every few years and replanted.

If you're going to place a beehive in the garden, join your local beekeeping association and get some lessons or expert assistance first.

GLOSSARY

Acid soil: This will have a pH lower than 7. It is suitable for acidic-soil-loving plants such as camellias and rhododendrons.

Alkaline soil: This soil has a pH ranging from 7 to 14. It is suitable for alkaline-soil-loving plants such as ceanothus, lavender, and choisya.

Annual plant: This is a plant that grows, flowers and dies all in one season. This is different to a perennial (see separate entry) that lives for a few years.

Brassica: These plants belong to the cabbage family. They include Brussels sprouts, kale, swede, kohlrabi, turnip, broccoli, and cauliflower.

Cloche: A cloche has two purposes. The main reason is to cover a plant to protect it from either the spring frosts or, later in the season, from cooler late autumn weather. However, they are also used to force plants on, by preventing light reaching them, to produce an earlier crop than usual. Most cloches are like mini polytunnels, using transparent plastic stretched over rows of vegetables. However, there are individual cloches that can be placed over plants as protection, which are traditionally bell-shaped and made of glass, although modern versions are usually plastic.

Deciduous: Refers to plants that lose their leaves when they go dormant, which is usually between mid October and mid spring. Plants that don't lose their leaves are called evergreen (see separate entry).

Drill: A drill is a very shallow trench, often only about ½ inch deep, into which vegetable or ornamental seeds are sown. Gardeners often use a string tied between two stakes to get a straight line and then use the edge of a hoe, or tip of a bamboo stake, to create the drill. After seed has been sown into the drill the soil should be gently pushed back, taking care not to disturb the seed.

Ericaceous: A term used by gardeners to describe either acidic soil or plants that prefer acidic soil, such as rhododendrons, camellias, and magnolias. The name is derived from the heather family, known as Erica, which prefers acidic conditions. It is suitable for plants that prefer a soil lower than a pH of about 6.5.

Evergreen: A type of plant that retains its leaves throughout the year. Despite the name, leaves don't have to be green, although most of them are. For example, a golden thyme would be referred to as evergreen. Plants that lose their leaves during cooler seasons are called deciduous (see separate entry).

Fleece: Horticultural fleece or frost cloth is often used to cover plants to protect them from the cold. It is usually white, and purchased on a roll which can be cut to size with scissors. It is then laid over vulnerable seedlings with the ends either being buried in soil or held down with bricks to stop it from blowing away. It is porous, meaning that it should allow rainwater to seep through and onto the seedlings.

Force on: This is a method used by gardeners to produce an earlier crop. A common example is rhubarb, where special terracotta "forcing" pots are used to cover the crowns in winter to force the stems to emerge a few weeks earlier than they otherwise would. Strawberries are also forced on early by placing a cloche over them or growing them in a greenhouse, resulting in an earlier crop by about two weeks.

Germination: When seeds break their dormancy and send out their first shoots and leaves, this is known as germination. The first leaves that are produced are known as cotyledons and the plant doesn't produce its "true" leaves until a few days later. When seeds germinate they also produce roots, which are then able to feed the growing plant.

Hardening off: Before planting seedlings directly outdoors after being grown indoors, young plants often need to be acclimatized so that the sudden changes of temperature don't kill them. Therefore gardeners often move them to a place which is cooler than the greenhouse but not as cold as directly outdoors, such as a cold frame or porch, and leave them there for a few days to toughen them up. This process is called hardening off.

Herbaceous plant: Refers to a plant which doesn't produce woody stems, so not a tree or a shrub. Most herbaceous plants will die back to below ground level during winter, but this isn't always the case, such as with hellebores. If the herbaceous plant is a perennial it will regrow from the root the following spring. Annual herbaceous plants simply die after the growing season.

Hugelkultur: A type of raised bed popular in Northern Europe, whereby soil is grown on top of decomposing wood, tree trunks, branches or other woody material. The theory is that the breaking down or rotting of the timber generates nutrients and retains moisture, creating a fertile environment for plants to grow in.

Keyhole gardening: A system originating in Africa but now popular internationally that is based on a raised bed shaped like a keyhole. In the center is a compost heap that gradually leaches out nutrients to the surrounding soil. It is a useful and sustainable method of creating a raised bed that should avoid the need for adding nutrients and reduces the amount of watering required.

Legume: A legume is a member of the pea and bean family. One of the benefits of growing them, apart from the delicious vegetables, is that members of this family fix nitrogen from the air into the soil, and then release it through their root systems. This means that after legumes have finished flowering and have been removed, the remaining ground should be rich in nitrogen, ideal for growing crops such as from the brassica family, without the need for adding fertilizers.

Mortar: This is a mix of sand, cement and water used to bond brickwork together. For bricklaying the ratio is usually three or four parts builders' sand to one part cement, but this varies between craftsmen.

Pan: A pan is a compacted area of soil where it is very difficult to grow plants as the root system is restricted. It can be broken up with a fork or mattock, but if the soil is very compacted this can be difficult. Raised beds offer a very useful solution to pans in the soil for a gardener.

Perennial plant: A plant that lives for more than two years, as opposed to an annual (see separate entry) that completes its life cycle in one year.

pH: This is the measurement used to determine whether something is acidic or alkaline. The scale is from 1 to 14, with the lower numbers being acidic and the higher numbers being alkaline. A pH of 7 is neutral. It is important for gardeners to know the pH of their soil as certain plants are fussy about what their growing conditions are.

Potting on: When a seedling or plant gets too big for its existing seed tray or pot, then it should be carefully removed and placed in a larger pot with more compost. This prevents the plant from becoming rootbound and gives the root system more space and a larger area to grow in, which should result in a larger and healthier plant.

Pricking out: This is a technique used by gardeners to remove seedlings when they're very young, before potting them on into a larger pot. There are small gadgets that can be used to "prick out," but thin plastic plant labels are just as useful to carefully lift out individual seedlings. It is usually advised that holding the stem should be avoided to prevent damaging it, and instead one of the leaves should be held to steady the plant.

Raised bed: Simply a growing space that is raised off the ground. Raised beds are usually made from bricks or timber, but people are often imaginative and recycle materials such as old bathtubs, sinks, or even rubber tyres and compost bags.

ADDITIONAL RESOURCES

Books

A Little Course in Growing Veg and Fruit
Simon Akeroyd
(DK, 2013)

All New Square Foot Gardening: The Revolutionary Way to Grow More In Less Space
Mel Bartholomew
(Cool Springs Press, 2013)

Allotment Handbook
Simon Akeroyd
(DK, 2013)

RHS Allotment Handbook
Simon Akeroyd, Geoff Hodge, Sara Draycott, Guy Barter
(Mitchell Beazley / RHS Publications, 2010)

The Good Gardener
Simon Akeroyd
(National Trust Books / Pavilion Books, 2015)

Complete Gardener's Manual
Simon Akeroyd, Zia Allaway, Helena Caldon, Martyn Cox, Jenny Hendy
(DK, 2011)

How to Grow Practically Everything
Zia Allaway and Lia Leendertz
(DK, 2010)

Design Ideas For Your Garden
Jacq Barber
(National Trust Books, 2013)

Fine Gardening Beds & Borders
Editors and Contributors of Fine Gardening
(The Taunton Press, 2012)

Fine Gardening Pocket Gardens
Editors and Contributors of Fine Gardening
(The Taunton Press, 2013)

The Fruit Gardener's Bible: A Complete Guide to Growing Fruits and Nuts in the Home Garden
Lewis Hill and Leonard Perry
(Storey Publishing, 2011)

How to Grow and Produce Your Own Food
Charles Boff
(Odhams Press Ltd, 1946)

RHS A–Z Encyclopedia of Garden Plants
Christopher Brickell
(DK / RHS Publications, 2008)

RHS Encyclopedia of Gardening
Christopher Brickell
(DK / RHS Publications, 2012)

RHS Simple Steps: Easy Pruning
Colin Crosbie
(DK, 2007)

Kitchen Garden Estate
Helene Gammack
(National Trust Books, 2012)

Encyclopedia of Flowering Shrubs
Jim Gardiner
(Timber Press, 2011)

The New Vegetable and Herb Expert
Dr D. G. Hessayon
(Expert Books, 2014)

RHS Grow Your Own Veg
Carol Klein
(Mitchell Beazley, 2010)

The Hillier Manual of Trees and Shrubs
Roy Lancaster and John Hillier
(RHS Publications, 2014)

Creative Vegetable Gardening
Joy Larkcom
(Mitchell Beazley, 1997)

Spade, Skirret and Parsnip: The Curious History of Vegetables
Bill Laws
(The History Press, 2004)

The New Kitchen Garden
Anna Pavord
(DK, 1996)

RHS New Encyclopedia of Gardening Techniques
(Mitchell Beazley, 2008)

Heritage Vegetables
Sue Stickland
(Gaia Books Ltd, 1998)

RHS Pests & Diseases
Pippa Greenwood and Andrew Halstead
(DK, 2009)

Straw Bale Gardens
by Joel Karsten
(Cool Springs Press, 2015)

Vertical Vegetables & Fruit: Creative Gardening Techniques for Growing Up in Small Spaces
Rhonda Massingham Hart
(Storey Publishing, 2011)

Websites

Missouri Botanical Garden Plant Finder
www.missouribotanicalgarden.org/plantfinder/plantfindersearch.aspx

USDA Plant Hardiness Zone Map
http://planthardiness.ars.usda.gov/PHZMWeb

Cooperative Extension Directory
http://nifa.usda.gov/partners-and-extension-map

Floridata
http://www.floridata.com

INDEX

INDEX

ACKNOWLEDGMENTS

I would like to thank the team at Quid for coming up with the concept for this book and was very flattered that they asked me to write it. I would particularly like to thank Lucy York for her patience while I scribbled away and for her dedication to producing a wonderful book, and James Evans for being such a great guy to work with.

I'd also like to thank my friend Simon Maughan from the RHS for being the consultant on this book and for offering fantastic advice. However, I would not like to thank him for suggesting that I should be photographed doing a step by step of making a wattle and daub raised bed in the traditional method, by using and mixing fresh cow manure by hand!

A massive thanks also to Vivien Henley for using her talented and creative photographic skills to take some wonderful shots of some of the raised beds featured in this book. And thank you for pinching my chocolates from my desk when I needed an energy boost the most!

I would also like to thank my springer spaniel Beanie for sitting patiently by my feet in the garden room, waiting for a walk each day, while I wrote yet another page of this book before taking her. And finally my wife Annabel and children Guy, Lissie, and Hugh for being so understanding while I locked myself away to write yet another book during spring and summer 2015… but I did buy you puppy River to say sorry. Hope it was worth it, kids!

ABOUT THE AUTHOR

Simon Akeroyd has written numerous horticultural books and articles for garden and lifestyle magazines and is a member of the Garden Media Guild.

He is Head Gardener for the National Trust and looks after the English Riviera portfolio, including Agatha Christie's Greenway, Coleton Fishacre, Compton Castle, and Bradley Manor. Prior to that he was a garden manager at RHS Wisley in Surrey and RHS Harlow Carr in North Yorkshire.

Simon worked for a few years for the BBC as a horticultural researcher and then producer, where he was involved in various projects such as the RHS Chelsea Flower Show and Hampton Court Palace Flower Show, and Gardeners' World. Apart from gardening, Simon is also a keen beekeeper. He lives by the sea in the Torbay area of South Devon.

IMAGE CREDITS